Deconstructing Group Work for Human Service Professionals

Spotlighting the skills of social group work, this handbook offers practical guidance and theoretical knowledge, enabling the reader to facilitate groups of varying types with increased clarity, purpose, and confidence. The reader is helped to understand what skill to employ, when, and why. New or veteran group facilitators are reminded to empower group members to both employ their strengths and engage in mutual aid – the fundamental value and methodology that underlies social group work. Specific skills help group members to coalesce as a cohesive group and optimize their capacity to reach their goals whether exploring therapeutic answers or accomplishing work tasks.

This book illustrates that there are "basics" to the method of human service work with groups that can help you to feel more at ease with and more effective at working with people in groups. The group work method is delineated for you, outlining: (1) skills of working with groups (ways of thinking or doing to make things happen), (2) practice principles (the moral reasoning that underlies what you choose to think and do in your practice), and (3) theoretical underpinnings for those choices (why your choices will achieve desirable ends). Anecdotal material and skills in action provide explicit examples of what skills look like in real time.

Social work students and academics as well as students and professionals working in the fields of youth work, counseling, mental health/clinical social work, and related health subjects will find this book of interest.

Dominique Moyse Steinberg, with a clinical background in child welfare and family service, has over 40 years of experience as educator, trainer, scholar, and researcher in social work with groups. She has practiced primarily in New York City and taught group work, research, and writing for publication at Hunter College, Smith College, and Simmons University School of Social Work. A certified professional mediator since 2000, Steinberg has also offered international workshops on addressing group conflict and catalyzing mutual aid. She has several research grants to her credit and is the author of many books and articles on group work process and values, research methods, and elder care.

Eileen C. Lyons, a social group worker by training, has dedicated her career to the youth development field, working in education, foster care, social work, and out-of-school time programs. Lyons' career includes 17 years as Executive Director of Interfaith Neighbors in NYC where she pioneered programs in literacy and bereavement. Lyons co-founded the journal *Afterschool Matters*, now published by the

National Institute on Out-of-School Time at the Wellesley Centers for Women. Since 2014, Lyons has held the position of Executive Director of Fresh Youth Initiatives, a community-based organization in Washington Heights that provides comprehensive social services and youth development programs to immigrant and first-generation children and their families.

Deconstructing Group Work for Human Service Professionals

A Skill-Building Handbook

Dominique Moyse Steinberg
and Eileen C. Lyons

Routledge
Taylor & Francis Group

LONDON AND NEW YORK

Cover image: © Getty Images

First published 2023
by Routledge
4 Park Square, Milton Park, Abingdon, Oxon OX14 4RN

and by Routledge
605 Third Avenue, New York, NY 10158

Routledge is an imprint of the Taylor & Francis Group, an informa business

British Library Cataloguing-in-Publication Data
A catalogue record for this book is available from the British Library

Library of Congress Cataloging-in-Publication Data
Names: Steinberg, Dominique Moyse, editor. | Lyons, Eileen C., editor.
Title: Deconstructing group work for human service professionals :
a skill-building handbook / edited by Dominique Moyse Steinberg
and Eileen C. Lyons.
Description: Milton Park, Abingdon, Oxon ; New York, NY : Routledge,
2023. | Includes bibliographical references and index. |
Identifiers: LCCN 2022020441 (print) | LCCN 2022020442 (ebook) |
ISBN 9780367433802 (hardback) | ISBN 9780367431280 (paperback) |
ISBN 9781003002789 (ebook)
Subjects: LCSH: Social group work. | Human services personnel.
Classification: LCC HV45 .D39 2023 (print) | LCC HV45 (ebook) |
DDC 361.4--dc23/eng/20220518
LC record available at https://lccn.loc.gov/2022020441
LC ebook record available at https://lccn.loc.gov/2022020442

ISBN: 978-0-367-43380-2 (hbk)
ISBN: 978-0-367-43128-0 (pbk)
ISBN: 978-1-003-00278-9 (ebk)

DOI: 10.4324/9781003002789

Typeset in Sabon
by KnowledgeWorks Global Ltd.

Contents

viii   *Contents*

Foreword

Welcome to this book on skills for working with groups; we are thrilled that you decided to pick it up! We have made some assumptions about people in the human services field who might benefit from a book on group work skills and what knowledge, expertise, and insights you are hoping to acquire. As group workers ourselves we experienced and listened to others as they experienced the highs and lows of the group work learning curve.

For us, group work is *bred in the bone*, a values-driven practice and a worldview. We hope that by introducing you to the social group work methodology and skills that guide our work, we can excite you about this particular brand of practice with groups. Group work becomes more satisfying, exciting, and effective when the worker employs skills with the precision of purpose, principle, and theory. We cannot offer you a road map, but we can provide the support that prepares you for the group work journey. For those of you who already facilitate groups with skill and confidence, this book can assist you to make explicit what may be implicit in your practice and better explain the integrity and importance of the work you do.

Perhaps what we both wish the most is that you enjoy reading this book about social work with groups as much as we enjoyed writing it!

Happy reading!

Dominique Moyse Steinberg and Eileen C. Lyons

Part 1

Introduction, Purpose, Context

Introduction

There are any numbers of reasons you may have picked up this book. Perhaps you already facilitate groups or teams on the job, and you are looking for a few pointers. Perhaps your supervisor just asked you to lead a group in your department, and you have no experience facilitating groups. Perhaps you are seeking immediate help for a crisis in your group. Or perhaps you facilitate the only groups in your work setting and are seeking common ground with other group workers.

Many human service workers report negative experiences in working with groups. Some practitioners facilitate groups in organizations in which there is no infrastructure and very little support for (if not outright opposition to) group work. Some believe that groups do not accomplish very much. Others believe that working with groups is just like working with individuals but multiplied, putting pressure on the worker to have an answer for everything (a proposition that often fails). Others – and this cohort may constitute the greatest number of practitioners – are anxious at the mere thought of working (or having to work) with groups for a whole host of reasons including the belief that it involves performing (and thus the possibility of making mistakes) in front of an audience.

If you approach working with groups with skepticism, ambivalence, or even trepidation, rest assured that whatever failures or inadequacies you have experienced, the failures are probably not yours! They are probably because you have not been introduced to specific skills, i.e., learned about the importance and impact of good planning in this era of multi-tasking at breakneck speed (Northen & Kurland 2001). Or perhaps you have been thrown to the wolves, by which we mean you have been asked to meet with a "bunch" of clients without any preparation – again, an issue of planning but also a scenario that reflects a real lack of understanding about groups and group work by your agency context. Or perhaps you have been asked to spend time with groups without any direction for what to do when you all come together. *These clients are all in trouble with the law*, says your supervisor. *The agency's job is to help them to stay out of trouble, and you might as well meet with all of them at once.*

Finally, you may lack a foundation for working with this method despite all the expectations placed on you. We are here – that is, this book is here – to tell you that working with groups is a method of professional human service and one that can be learned in any number of ways! The method has been developed from years

DOI: 10.4324/9781003002789-1

of formal and informal study, and it consists of many skills that can be learned (Schwartz & Berman-Rossi (1990); Brandler & Roman 2015; Breton 2006; Coyle 1946; Garvin 1997; Hartford 1971 and 1978; Henry 1992; Konopka 1963 and 1964, Kurland 2007, Lang 2010; Middleman & Wood 1990b, Newstetter 1935; Northen & Kurland 2001; Papell & Rothman 1966; Phillips 1954 and 1957; Schwartz 2005; Schwartz & Zalba 1971; Shulman 2012; Steinberg 2014a; Toseland & Rivas 2017; Trecker 1955; Zastrow & Hessenauer 2019).

Whatever category or stance in which you find yourself, the goal of this book is to illustrate for you that there are "basics" to the method of human service work with groups that can go a long way in helping to make you more at ease with and more effective at – and even further, delighted at the idea of – working with people in groups. This package, which we call *method* and which is delineated in this book for you, includes the following: (1) *skills of working with groups* (ways of thinking or doing to make things happen), (2) *practice principles* (the moral reasoning that underlies what you choose to think and do in your practice), and (3) *theoretical underpinnings for those choices* (why your choices will achieve desirable ends). These three elements of professional group work, when combined, lift workers from a mechanical or purely intuitive mindset to a professional mindset (Coyle 1946; Dewey 1910; Middleman & Wood 1990a; Northen & Kurland 2001; Schwartz 2005; Steinberg 2014a). For example, group workers usually position chairs for a group meeting in a circle – either mechanically because that is how everyone does it – or professionally, because one knows that it creates an expectation of belonging, of being a part of something, an emerging safe space in which group members can see one another and create and share norms, purpose, and ultimately, ownership of the group. To paraphrase a well-known and highly-esteemed group work scholar, William Schwartz, social service encounters may be just a moment long in the lives of many folks, but the power of that momentary encounter is enormous in its capacity for ripple effect (that is, in its capacity to help in a profound way) when the practitioner enters it with *skill* (Schwartz & Berman-Rossi 1990).

People who train in social group work are often excited by the notion that at some point they will be "skilled" in the work. They may also begin the journey by wondering what in the world that will look like. What is a skill, exactly, they ask, assuming there is some mystery to unravel. As they move along the learning process, they come to see, as will you, that with few exceptions, skills are nothing more than ways of thinking or behaving with which we are probably already familiar but that are re-conceptualized as "skill" in order to understand and define a particular form of professional behavior (Berman-Rossi 1993; Henry 1992; Brandler & Roman 2015; Middleman & Wood 1990a; Northern & Kurland 2001; Phillips 1954 and 1957; Schwartz 2005; Shulman 2012; Steinberg 2014a). That is, certain behaviors with which you may be familiar are transformed from "behavior" to "skill" once they are considered in full context, a context that has three components:

1 Their purpose (intent/what the skill hopes to accomplish),
2 The principle (moral compass) that it reflects, and
3 The theory in which its application is rooted (a chain of ideas that when connected, explains why the particular skill gets you to a desired goal).

This book on skills of group work practice aims to help you to get into this mindset in every aspect of your thinking and behaving, and to that end you will be helped to do the following:

1 *Understand the nature of a skill in terms of its intent*, generally understood as wishing to advance a group's process from *pre-planning* (what kind of group to consider and why) to *post-termination* (life for members after the group ends). It also includes your behavior both in (as in meeting with prospective members) and outside of the group (as in talking with agency staff about your ideas).
2 *Understand the principles of practice that undergird the skills* we offer here (what each skill [behavior] is trying to achieve) and especially as intent reflects democratic and humanistic values (Glassman & Kates 1990) in order to enhance your professionalism and prevent your practice from being inadvertently oppressive (Caplan & Thomas 2003; Kurland & Salmon 1990; Lee 2001; Malekoff, Salmon, & Steinberg 2006; Trecker 1955). As noted earlier, principles reflect the moral compass for working with people and help to prevent action that is haphazard and results that are disastrous.
3 *Transfer your skills to any group in which you work* by offering for each skill the theoretical underpinnings that explain the relationship between what you do and outcome – *why* a given skill helps you to get where you want to go (e.g., the group needs to think more broadly, the group needs to plan an event, an individual needs to speak up more, the group needs to address its purpose, the group needs to deal with conflict). As noted earlier, once you know the theoretical underpinning of a skill, your practice moves from mechanical or rote to professional (Bernstein 1973; Coyle 1946; Northen & Kurland 2001; Steinberg 2014a). At that point, you are able to articulate why you do what you do in your practice.

Additional to this package are two special pieces of content that we hope will round out the guidance we offer. First, attached to each skill we present a *sidebar*, a short example of the skill in action. Learning about a particular way of being with a group is one thing, but examples bring skills to life. Second, to round out the discussion of each skill, we offer an *essay*, a longer narrative that elaborates on the skill in the context of work, be it in the group with members or outside of the group with significant others such as agency management or family or community members. The next section explains the purpose of this book as we see it.

Why This Book

The purpose of this book on skills for working with groups is to help people who work with groups to do a good job. What we mean by a "good job" is to effectively employ certain skills that help any group to achieve its purpose for existing, however that purpose is defined. Some groups are formed to carry out certain tasks; some are intended to educate; some are formed to provide support for the vagaries of life. Whatever the reason, the hope is that being a member of a group is therapeutic regardless of its purpose – that is, that people who join and participate in any group will find it satisfying.

As noted earlier, some people who work with groups without benefit of specialized education in the method or training often think that working with groups is really just a matter of working with a number of individuals at the same time, so they think, *what's the big deal*? That is, what's the big deal until they actually sit in a circle with those individuals, say six or seven of them, whose eyes are all focused on them. That is, in fact, the big deal. Without knowing that there are skills specific to working with groups, those workers are left in a lurch. *Where and how to begin? And once I begin, then what?* All of a sudden, the burden seems heavy and growing, and with this mindset in place, there are, in fact, a few "big deals."

First, being in the presence of "a number of individuals at once" in the role of group facilitator inevitably makes one feel that one is performing for an audience. Of course, this is going to make you nervous! Second, feeling solely responsible for helping the people in the group can seem daunting; to help or guide or advise or even just support one person can be challenging, but to do so with or for a number of people all at once – and in front of others, no less – can be positively daunting. Finally, anticipating the unknown – an untold number of things that members might say or do ... or alternatively, facing the stillness of a group in which no one talks, can rouse anxiety in the least controlling among us (no less in those of us who prefer a script). Hence, fear of groups and group work.

What we hope is that this book will help you to see a few things more clearly from a group work perspective. First, group work is not about performing. The idea that the group worker must perform is a factor in practice only if the worker assumes sole responsibility for what happens in and to the group. This kind of stance, however, means that all of the strengths (skills, talents, experience, know-how, and other forms of savvy) that people bring with them to the group remain hidden and untapped. One must wonder, then, why even bother to have people together at the same time and place? Does that not just waste the time of all those who watch? what happens between worker and one member (at a time)? Could their time not be better spent doing something else?

In a nutshell, then, if the role of the group worker is to perform, then the role of group members must be to receive – like an audience, recipients of service without participation. This kind of relationship between group worker and group members is tremendously wasteful of all energy by ignoring all that group members might lend to one another. Further, it can set the stage for power struggles between the worker who has all the power and members who have usually little to none, often leading to oppressive practice (keeping members in line) as the worker struggles to remain in control. Even further, it also sets the stage for power struggles among the members, who must vie for that personal touch (time, space, attention) from the worker.

Finally, and once again closely related, if the worker is the performer, then the worker is responsible (as in any traditional performance) for both success (should that be the happy outcome) and failure (more often the case in this kind of scenario), a truly exhausting approach to human service! No wonder so many people are group shy; the mere idea of having to perform is daunting. Bad enough to try to help one person successfully, but the idea of having to perform over and over again in front of an audience of six or eight people (which, in the world of human service, usually means to perform some kind of problem-solving magic) makes one want to lie down and forget the whole thing!

What we suggest as an alternative mindset or approach to practice is one of shared responsibility – that is, everyone in a group is responsible for everything that takes place in the group, good or bad. The worker assumes the role of *educator* (rather than performer) who helps members to share responsibility by identifying desirable norms, values, and behaviors as the group moves along; thus, the other participants become co-creators of the kind of group process that will move the group's work, however defined, to its end goal in a positive, productive, and hopefully enjoyable and rewarding way. In this scenario the pressures on the worker are (1) to understand the dynamics of planning and forming a group with the best possible chance of success and (2) to educate group members as they carry out their work.

Part 2 of this book offers definitions of key terms we use throughout this book just to make sure that all of us, authors and users, understand the concepts in the same way. Part 2 also identifies the values that underlie the approach to group work that we offer you, discusses the underlying assumptions we make in developing the content of this book, describes how the book is organized, and offers a few words about the professional literature that supports and directs our approach to group work.

Part 2
The Basics of Group Work Method and Skill

We begin this section with definitions of key terms that represent concepts to which we refer throughout the book. While some may seem self-evident, we provide our definitions to make sure we are on a common page as we describe, discuss, and offer suggestions about practice.

The next section discusses the major values that we hold for human service generally and that drive our approach to professional group work practice. These values form the foundation for everything that we offer and suggest to you in this book. The following section identifies the major assumptions that we made in both our thinking that there was a need for this book and thus in constructing the content of this book. That is followed by a brief overview of how this book is organized and a final few words about our use of professional literature and suggestions for further reading.

Definitions of Key Terms

We have made every attempt to refrain from the kind of jargon intended to exclude, but there are some key terms of the group work method that require a common understanding. Definitions of key terms follow.

Groups

For purposes of this conversation, we propose a *group* to be composed of three or more people who come together on purpose or if not on purpose, then who either find one (*We are here at this time in this place; what might be our purpose?*) or inherently have a common purpose for meeting together (*We are mandated to meet as a group because of certain problems; let us form a group purpose around addressing those problems*). Also, heads up! Two people does not a "grouplet" make, as has been heard in some quarters, and a gathering of 20 people is not what we have in mind when we speak about groups, at least not in this book.

Clearly, groups vary greatly in number (as well as other ways), and we propose that an optimal number is between four and eight depending on context and purpose. What you want to avoid is ending up with only two people in a session because one person is absent or having so many people present in each meeting that it is impossible for everyone's voice to be heard in a meaningful way. This means that in considering the upper range of numbers, you want to also consider the length of time of each meeting. For example, a group of eight people has more time for each voice in a two-hour meeting than a one-hour meeting. Thus, optimally speaking, you want

DOI: 10.4324/9781003002789-2

enough people so that the group is both stimulated and stimulating but not so many that members are routinely excluded from participating because of time issues. This is especially relevant if you are seeking any depth of conversation.

Group Purpose

The one constant, we believe, that truly defines group work as we understand it, it is that people achieve their goals best when they come together with (or immediately develop) a common explicitly stated purpose, which refers to some common cause to which they all relate even if the specific needs or issues that bring them to the group differ. Thus, a group of parents might all have children who are not doing very well in school, albeit in different ways, but the fact that their children are having trouble in school constitutes the needs that drive the group's common purpose, one to which they all relate. One parent might need help with helping a child improve study habits, while another parent might need help with ideas for helping a child make friends, while yet another parent might need the group to offer ideas for helping a child be less afraid to ask questions in class. While their individual goals pertaining to how to help their children vary, the group purpose of helping their children to do better is the thread that binds them together – that helps them to relate to one another and as the group moves along. The concept of group purpose (the why of a group) is so important to social group work that an entire skill set in Part 3 is devoted to deconstructing it into its various skills.

Group Work

By *group work* we mean purposeful thoughts and actions of the worker that are intended to help a group to form and carry out its work however that work is defined. Those thoughts and actions might take place in a meeting but might also take place outside of meetings. For example, speaking to potential members constitutes group work in that it is intended to discover if a group might be useful and what kind of group might be desired. Speaking to agency representatives, such as administrators, program directors, and colleagues also constitutes group work in that it aims to discover the context's history and experience with groups – what has been tried, how groups and group work are viewed by the system, or whether colleagues are likely to help or hinder the process. In short, any and all actions that aim to get a group off the ground, aim to help a group to form and conduct its affairs, and that aim to help members to transit to life after group is *group work*.

We are very specific in our use of the term *group work* on two bases. First, we use the term *group work* rather than leadership, because we believe that true group work requires shared and flexible leadership. The worker may take the lead in some meetings, such as when a group begins, but if members are to be actively involved in helping one another to meet their goals, which we believe is integral to group work, then they too must have the freedom to lead on occasion, such as offering ideas or suggestions or even different ways of seeing things. Thus, our vision of group work includes the invitation, encouragement, and promotion of internal leadership at many, if not most, moments.

Second, we refer to working with groups rather than running groups, because running in the context of human service makes no sense. Does one ever run an individual? Hopefully not!

If one does, then one is basically mirroring the oppression that may already take place in that person's life. Additionally, to run something connotes a degree of power, if not absolute power. However, absolute power is the very opposite of shared or flexible leadership, a fundamental value of group work that we believe can and should be practiced. In contrast to running a group, *working with* a group is a way of participating in a group that assumes the value of and promotes shared responsibility for all of a group's affairs, including its successes. It demands that everyone in a group step up to the plate whenever it is thought that a step-up could advance the group's work. *In it together* is the motto of this approach, a much more relaxed, relaxing, and joyful way of working!

Practitioner

We use this term to refer to everyone who works directly with people in the human-service field regardless of degree. Thus, if you work in human service and directly with people, then the term "practitioner" refers to you.

Group Worker

We use the term *group worker* rather than leader or facilitator to underscore the fact that the service one provides when serving people in groups is work. As noted above, we believe that leadership in any group should be both shared (not only the purview of a formal convener) and flexible (move from participant to participant according to any given moment). Finally, logic suggests that if we call service to groups *group work*, then the person offering the service is a *group worker*.

The Worker as Educator

In the approach to group work we offer you here, the worker's primary role is that of *educator* (Kurland & Salmon 1993), and you will see this as one of the skills that we identify. To educate in this context means to help the members of a new group to: (1) learn the ropes of good group citizenship, (2) maintain their hold on those ropes as their work encounters new territory (as in, *Uh oh, we have our first conflict; now what?*), and (3) transfer what they have learned (new ways of being, doing, and thinking) from this group into the other groups to which they belong in their daily lives.

   This way of conceptualizing the group worker recognizes the formal convener as having an expertise in group methods and dynamics. The group worker is in a good position to suggest ways of being, doing, and thinking in the group that will best help to propel it forward. Note that it does not conceptualize the worker as being a particular expert in the material or subject (life situations, problems, concerns) that brings the members together. Rather, it recognizes that people are, with few exceptions, experts in their own lives and that it is precisely that savvy, gleaned from both their successes and failures, that they can lend to others as the group experience attempts to help them to all reach their goals (Breton 2006; Kurland & Salmon 1990 and 1993; Lee 2001; Steinberg 2014a). In this practice scenario, then, the worker has an area of expertise related to advancing desirable norms and values and to helping the group to develop and to maintain a democratic and humanistic tone (Glassman & Kates 1990).

Practice

Generally, when we speak of *practice* in this book, we are referring to any and all professional actions that aim to carry out human-service work. Given the purpose of this book, we mean professional actions that help you to conceptualize, plan, form, intervene with, and follow-up with groups or their members. In short, anything you do that is professionally based and aims to advance your service to people in groups, we refer to as your practice. Now that you recognize your practice, you can also describe yourself as a practitioner!

Skills

As already noted, a *skill* is a behavior or an act or action of some kind that is carried out purposefully. A thinking behavior such as telling a group that the meeting is about to end and asking members to review that day's process to prepare for the next meeting. In either case, these are skills because they are carried out with purpose.

Good news! If you have ever worked with groups, you already have an enormous array of skills. Glance through the skills that we have identified in Part 3 to discover them. Now you just need to rethink them *from* what you do in an ordinary-everyday-sort-of-way *to* the purposeful behavior you employ to reach a certain goal (e.g., to help the group meet its needs [do the work] of the moment, whatever the task and goal and however small [arranging chairs] or large [helping a member to address a problem outside of the group]).

Group-Specific Skills

Understanding the group as system is essential in order to understand the concept of *group-specific* skill. A group is a system in much the same way we normally understand the concept of system, with members taking on various roles (as do the various parts of any system, such as a machine). They take on responsibilities, exercise certain strengths, and attempt to meet their individual needs, all working on their own behalf while simultaneously contributing to the functioning of that system (all parts of a machine working together to make that machine do what it is supposed to do). In the language of systems, this kind of process is often referred to as one consisting of (1) inputs; in group work jargon we refer to inputs as the skills, talents, and needs that individual members bring; (2) throughputs; in group work jargon we refer to this as the process that takes place when the members come together, also referred to as its "work;" and (3) outputs; in group work jargon we speak of members' accomplishments. In fact, it is this kind of thinking – seeing a group as a system – that often has trained professionals talking about the magic of groups, their ability to make two plus two equal five or, as often stated, their potential to become greater than the sum of their parts. In fact, *strength in numbers*, a well-known potential of groups and one of the nine mutual-aid dynamics we present in this book reflects this very idea (see skill set on mutual aid, pp. 80–90).

Group-specific skill, then, is a body of behaviors that focuses on the group as system rather than on the individual members. Naturally, a skill may be directed to an individual, but that is on behalf of the group. For example, noticing that a member has raised an eyebrow (a form of communication, we believe) would cause the group worker to say to the group in general, *I just noticed that Sue has raised an eyebrow. Mmm …* That the worker said this to the group system, however (as in, *I noticed that one of your parts just did something in particular*) rather than to the individual (as in, *I noticed, Sue, that you just raised an eyebrow*) makes the intervention *group specific*.

People who are untrained in a group work may not realize that the group work method contains certain skills that are *group specific*. As just noted, by group specific we mean that they consist of behaviors that are appropriate (and necessary) for working with groups but not relevant to working with an individual and that are always concerned with the interactional quality and impact of what is going on (how every member's presence affects every other member's presence). Thus, when we are taught to understand groups as systems with integral and intricate parts (in a human group the members constituting those parts), we immediately see that two entities exist at the same time: (1) the individual members, who have come together for some reason and (2) the totality of those individuals, also known as the group (or group *system*).

Here are three concrete examples of *group-specific* skills. First is the skill of *scanning* (Middleman & Wood 1990). Scanning refers to looking around the group when the worker speaks and listens. The intent of this skill is to make sure that all types of communication (body language such as eye rolling, yawning, signs of wishing to speak/interject, etc.) are noticed and invited into the mix of discussion. One would never consider scanning when working with an individual. Can you imagine what the other person would think if your eyes were to wander around the room as you spoke or as you listened to that person speak? In the case of listening, people might assume you were bored and in the case of speaking, one can only imagine the many possible reactions! Thus, scanning is definitely a group-specific skill, very appropriate for group work.

A second example is the skill, *think group*. The label alone identifies it as a behavior that is group rather than individual oriented. As we explain and elaborate on pages 55 and 56, to *think group* is to think of having two clients in mind when working with a group, the first being the collection of individuals gathered together (meaning that each individual's needs and contributions receive our attention) and the second being the group as a system (meaning our consideration of the group as a whole). This is why we might speak of group members, but we also speak of "the group" as a single unit – how the group is doing, where the group is meeting, what the group's focus is, and what its goals and accomplishments are, for example. To *think group*, then, means to offer attention beyond that which we give to each individual. In order that individual members are not lost in that shuffle (or vice versa), the worker maintains an eye on both the group as system and its individual members, which takes practice and requires the engagement of another skill, dual focus.

The skill of *dual focus* comes from the world of equestrianism and in that idiom is referred to as "hard eye soft eye" (Steinberg 2014a). However you refer to it this skill connotes simultaneous attention to two spheres. In the world of equestrianism one sphere (hard eye) is the path on which the horse and rider are engaged. One eye, literally, needs to be on that path to make sure that there are no obstacles (a snake, for example). The other eye, literally, needs to be on the surrounding environment to make sure that the larger context for the ride is also safe. Thus, hard eye

(eye on the immediate) and soft eye (eye on the larger perimeter) maintain a dual focus for the rider, helping to ensure a smooth ride. In group work this concept is translated as *dual focus*, meaning one of the worker's "eyes" is always on each individual member in the group (how each is faring at all times), and one "eye" is always on the group as a whole (how the group is faring at all times). In this mindset each member is integral to helping the group "machine" to stay in good working order, and the group "machine" is integral to helping each part [member] remain well-oiled [given the attention required] in order for all goals to be met.

The skills of scanning, thinking group, and dual focus do not apply to individual work but are integral to group work. It is unlikely that a practitioner who is untrained in social group work will know about them. Of course, many skills used in the practice of group work are generic and can be either used similarly in work with individuals (such as assessment skills) or transposed for use from one to the other (such as sessional-ending skills, which have one look in group work and another in individual work but both of which aim to transit from one work session to the next).

Principles

Essentially, a principle is a general belief that you have about the way people should behave with one another, a belief that influences what you say and do. Thus, it contains a moral element and reflects your values: *one should act in a certain way in this circumstance.*

Principles contained in theories or various philosophies are their basic rules – rules regarding ways of being and doing things (Northen 2006; Trecker 1955). For example, a political ideology will have certain principles that guide those who attempt to enact that ideology in society. In some contexts you might refer to a principle as a standard or rule of conduct or even an attitude. What all of these contexts have in common, however, is that their principles include a moral component, or a "should" factor.

For example, several group work skills we offer note the principle of self-determination. Thus, the concept of self-directed action is the *raison d'être* of that skill. In other words, we believe that making something happen (the goal of the skill in question) should respect and promote a fundamental right of people to determine their destiny. Hence, self-determination is the principle on which the skill is based.

Theory

At its most basic level a theory is a chain of ideas that when conceptually connected (Idea A plus Idea B and maybe plus Idea C) either describe or prescribe something. In the context of this book, a short theoretical proposition presented as an "if-then" explanation is offered for each skill in order to give you the "why" of the behavior. In short, the intent of the proposition is to offer you the following: *If you carry out Skill X then you will achieve Goal Y.* When you review the skills, you will see that we offer this for each skill.

It is this understanding – of the *why* of something – that will allow you to articulate an informed answer to others who ask, *Why did you do such and such?* Imagine a student intern (or a supervisor) sitting in on your group session and asking you that question. Without theory to back you up you are acting mechanically, able only to do what you are told (as in, *I did it because I was told to* or *because I saw So and So do it* or *because we always do it this way*) but unable to answer why. However, once you understand the theoretical foundation for what you do, you can say, *I did that because I thought it would help the group to accomplish X.*

Mutual Aid

Mutual aid refers to the process of people helping one another (Steinberg, 2014a). The type of helping that falls under the rubric of mutual aid is extensive. Mutual aid, as both a concept and a concrete interactional process, is discussed in the section that addresses its various skill components (see pp. 80–90). However, because it is so central to our way of thinking about and working with groups, it warrants a brief introductory narrative at this early point in the book, and here is a brief introduction to the nature, role, and importance of mutual aid in working with groups.

> **Dynamic #1: sharing information.** People can help one another by sharing knowledge, ideas, wisdom, experience, feelings, perspectives, and their special skills and talents.
> **Dynamic #2: debating differences.** People can help one another by comparing and contrasting different ways of being, doing, or thinking.
> **Dynamic #3: talking about taboo subjects.** People can help one another by allowing discussions of topics that are not normally welcome in general or "polite" society.
> **Dynamic #4: being in the same boat.** People can help one another just by being in the company of others who they believe understand how they think and feel.
> **Dynamic #5: mutual support.** People can help one another by offering sympathy (*I've been in your shoes*) or empathy (*I've not been where you are, but I've felt the way I think you feel*).
> **Dynamic #6: mutual demand.** People can help one another by demanding that any given moment requiring energy, thought, and focus be taken seriously.
> **Dynamic #7: individual problem solving.** People can help one another by offering problem-solving brain power.
> **Dynamic #8: rehearsal.** People can help one another as sounding boards for practicing new ways of thinking, being, or doing.
> **Dynamic #9: strength in numbers.** People can help one another by lending many voices to action.

In the introduction to the related skill set (see p. 80), we offer a more detailed overview of mutual aid as a foundation for strength-based practice.

Underlying Values

In this book, we propose a group work method that advances certain values. We offer them here in alphabetical order, finding it impossible to grade and thus order them in terms of importance.

Commitment

We value commitment on the part of every group participant. Indicators of a member's commitment include open self-reflection, being on time, listening, sharing thoughts, and both making and being receptive to demands for serious attention to the work. In our approach to group work commitment extends beyond self-help to helping fellow members to reach their stated goals and to sharing in the responsibility for the group's well-being (such as participating in the management of group affairs so that they are thoughtful, purposeful, and effective).

Consensus/Democracy

While democracy seems to be the most humane way for large groups to govern, we believe that small groups should strive for consensus. Consensus refers to 100% agreement about a decision and thus, discourages the limited option of winners and losers that voting prescribes. We recognize the value of voting as a decision-making method in a large group; a group of 40 may have difficulty achieving true consensus. We believe, however, that in a climate of good will, respect, and perhaps a bit of creative thinking, a group of eight does have a good chance of reaching consensus. Why choose the time-consuming process of reaching consensus over quick and easy voting? Experience indicates that a frequent upshot of voting in a small group is the occurrence of hard feelings in the aftermath – feelings of being unheard and devalued by those who "lost" the vote. In contrast, while working to achieve consensus does take time, it creates an opportunity for advancing group cohesion and growth. Specifically, consensus-building requires group members to work together toward a solution (through discussion, compromise, listening, and understanding) that is acceptable to (if not perfect for) everyone; it further draws on everyone's skills and strengths in the process (group work at its best), and feels like a shared success when consensus is finally reached. Implicit in this value is the related value of *voice*.

Difference as Enriching

We value the potential for differences of all types to be enriching (Northen 2002; Steinberg 2014a). We believe that conflict is an expression of difference (see the related skill set, pp. 91–101) with the potential to deepen and broaden people's shared understanding, empathy, and insights and over the long term, to strengthen all sorts of relationships for the better. Thus, our approach to work with groups embraces the expression of difference when it arises in a group and has an aim of helping members to maintain a climate of good will, as they exercise (or perhaps improve) good articulation and listening skills.

Empowerment

Providing opportunities for group members to reach for and achieve their potential, personal goals, and vision is central to this group work approach (Bernstein 1962 and 1973, Breton 2006; Galinsky & Schopler 1971; Lee 2001; Lietz 2007; Northen 2006; Roman 2002; Steinberg 2014a). Providing opportunities for people to participate in shaping and constructing a group that meets their needs also constitutes empowerment. Thus, a worker's main tasks in this regard are (1) to be explicit about the value of empowerment, (2) to help the group to work toward achieving its purpose, and (3) to purposefully and actively step aside as often as possible to give members enough space to exercise their voices, exchange their strengths, and share in authority over group affairs. Finally, as noted earlier in two other stated values, also implicit in the value of empowerment is the value of *voice*, that is the need for, importance of, and right of people to exercise their voices in ventures that touch them in any way.

Humanism

By humanism we mean that human beings are in the world together, with no one more fundamentally "worthy" than another, and all entitled to basic respect and dignified treatment (Glassman & Kates 1990).

Holistic Thinking

By holistic thinking we mean that in any professional encounter in human-service work, the "whole" of a person should be considered, not just the needy or broken parts (Breton 2006). Strengths (skills and talents) should be incorporated into the development of any helping path (Breton 2006; Steinberg 2014a). This emphasis on strengths is supported by many skills (Middleman & Wood 1990b) that aim to help group members to help one another rather than turn to the worker as expert helper. Inherent in this value is the value of mutual aid, a "collection" of specific ways in which people in groups can help one another (Steinberg 2014a).

Knowledge

We value knowledge and the strength that knowledge gives to those who hold it. This value is advanced in groups by ensuring opportunities for group members to become informed and to share their knowledge in the group. As the saying goes, *knowledge is power*. If you review all of the values identified here, you will quickly see that they all reflect empowerment in one way or another.

Self-Determination

We value every person's right to shape (or in some cases such as with children, to participate in shaping) their destiny. In group work the worker communicates this value to group members by stating that all participants are expected to actively contribute to helping the group to carry out its work, however defined (Bernstein 1962; Caplan & Thomas 2003; Galinsky & Schopler 1972; Mullender & Ward 1991; Schopler & Galinsky 1981). Once again, implicit in this value is the related value of *voice*.

Transparency

We value straightforward and honest relationships between practitioners and clients. In group work this translates into refraining from ever having a hidden agenda with a group. A hidden agenda is a scenario in which the worker forms a group for a particular purpose without being honest and open about that purpose with potential or prospective group members. Hidden agendas often leave group members to flounder in the group process because the worker has not in fact shared real expectations or actual purpose (Bernstein 1962, 1973 and 1993; Northen & Kurland 2001).

Underlying Assumptions

In writing this book, we have made a few major assumptions about you, the reader, which we now share with you in the service of providing as much transparency about our thinking as possible.

Modifying Practice

We assume that you are both open to and able to review, modify, and enhance your current approach to working with groups. If the setting in which you practice does not readily lend itself to all of the recommendations that we offer but you are interested in what we say in this book, we assume that you will search for "wiggle" room to implement at least some of our ideas in ways that are not blatantly contradictory to the service philosophy of your setting. We present an ideal, assume that you will do what you can, and hope that you will act as both ambassador and educator in your work setting to help your peers and other relevant agency staff to better understand the basics of social group work.

Professional Development

We assume that you are interested in ongoing professional development to support your practice and as we discuss a bit more later, hope that you will peruse some of our citations and current professional journals. Interest in professional development also means to us that if opportunities arise for training (e.g., attending or presenting your work at conferences), you will consider taking advantage of those opportunities. Finally, it means that you will attempt to share any new knowledge and ideas that you may glean from using practice suggestions we offer in this book with anyone and everyone else who might benefit from that knowledge, such as supervisors, colleagues, interns, and other related professionals.

Professional Values

While we would like to assume that you are already or will become interested in the practice values that we emphasize, we can only really say that we hope that you will do so. That said, we do assume that when you work with people in groups you are interested in projecting authority that comes from professional savvy and not professional power. We propose an approach to practice in this book that assumes a greater interest in *serving* the needs of others than in imposing personal values (which we see as constituting oppressive practice) and thus hope that you are interested in promoting the values that we outlined earlier and that we believe are expressed through the skills we present. We further assume that you value transparency (that is, helping people to understand your thinking) so that you are open to reflection and criticism by others, including and perhaps even most particularly the people you wish to serve. Translated into action, this means that we assume that you do (or will after reading this book) approach your practice with no hidden agenda (see Appendix B, *On Hidden Agendas*) but rather in an open and curious mindset of good will. Finally, we assume that you are interested in and will thus engage in professional evaluation of your practice at all possible opportunities in order to continue enhancing what you do and how you do it.

How This Book Is Organized

We believe that we have organized Part 3 (the skills section of this book) in a way that allows you to enter the conversation at any number of entry points. You can select skills in any order and read from there. For example, you might start with what sings to you – what feels most compelling and relevant. We strongly recommend, however, that you read the introductory content first as context, because Parts 1 and 2 explain how we see group work, why we offer a book that deconstructs its major skills, and offer definitions of frequently used terms to ensure a common understanding as you read Part 3.

The format of Part 3 is as follows. It begins by identifying a skill (a very few words denoting a way of being, doing, or thinking), offers a sentence of elaboration on that skill, identifies a principle that reflects the value or moral precept inherent in that skill, and proposes a brief theoretical rationale for using the skill. As noted earlier, each skill is also accompanied by a brief *sidebar* that offers an example of the skill in action and an *essay* that elaborates on the use of the skill either in a group context or on behalf of a group you are planning or with which you are already working.

It is important to remember that as with any complex system, the deconstruction of skills is in the service of clarity and increased understanding. There are, in fact, multiple instances of overlap among all of the skills. In other words, many skills have more than one aim, as you will come to understand once you engage with them and begin to experience their results. We have elected to focus on the primary aim of each skill in order to offer what we hope is a clear and relatively simple path for adopting it.

A Word About Professional Literature

Our work (our various practices including administration, teaching, research, scholarship, and direct clinical services) is built, as the saying goes, on the shoulders of people we think of as giants in our field. Because much of what we offer here is rooted in fundamental theories of social group work, which originated and abounded throughout the last century, you will likely have some reaction to some of the dates of our citations! Yes, admittedly, some of the literature we have included in citations dates way, way back! However, the literature we chose to include that does date far back into the previous century, does in fact represent the giants of our field who laid the foundation for professional practice today and thus, in theoretical terms, is as relevant today as it was many yesterdays ago when it was first written.

Some of this literature is complex, but much of it is quite accessible, and we encourage you, if at all possible, to pursue any of it that piques a particular interest area. In addition, we urge you to access (perhaps ask your agency to subscribe to) the journals that are most germane to work with groups today. Those are *Social Work with Groups* (USA), *Groupwork* (UK), and *Small Group Research* (USA). These can be all found online as well as in various types of libraries in hard copy. Finally, we encourage you to visit the primary website for social work with groups, the *International Association for Social Work with Groups*. This membership association is based in the United States but represents group workers and related interested professionals from all over the world and offers an annual conference as well.

On to Part 3, which offers you what we hope will be a body of skills for working with groups that will help you to enhance your practice, enhance your professionalism, and allow you to work with groups in a joyful, productive, and satisfying way.

Part 3

The Skills of Group Work Deconstructed

Introduction

Part 3 offers suggestions for strength-based group work skill sets in six key categories:

Unit 1: Need
Unit 2: Purpose
Unit 3: Worker Role
Unit 4: Group Process
Unit 5: Catalyzing Mutual Aid
Unit 6: Addressing Conflict

Each unit begins with an introduction, a roster of skills, and a list of major concepts addressed in that set. The skill is identified, followed by a one-sentence elaboration, the principle in which we believe the skill is rooted, and a brief theoretical statement that we believe provides justification for the skill. Each skill also offers a *sidebar* that presents an example of the skill in action. To round out the context for practicing that particular skill we then offer an *essay*, which elaborates on the role, importance, and use of the skill. In some cases, the essay may be followed by what we call *differential application* when we think the skill is exercised in so many varied and distinctive contexts that it warrants further elaboration.

As noted elsewhere, there is inevitable overlap of both the skill's intent and action across the categories, but you will see that the examples we offer attempt to place each skill in a particular context, which we hope will help to make the points about the widely-varying utility of each skill.

DOI: 10.4324/9781003002789-3

Unit 3:1 Skill Set
Need

Overview

In this section on need-based skills you are introduced to skills that will enable you to identify needs of the population with which you work, to consider needs in organizational and social/political contexts, and to recognize the evolving and dynamic nature of needs. We hope you will internalize and appreciate the guiding axiom that in group work, *the concept of need drives all thinking about group purpose*. In the broader context of this approach, you will be introduced to the concept of mutual aid, which speaks to the concrete ways in which people who come together with a common need guided by an agreed-upon purpose can help one another. When mutual aid dominates the group process as it does in social group work, the worker's essential set of skills is to orchestrate conversation among members in such a way that they look for, reach for, and lend their skills and talents to one another in order to meet the needs (or desires) that brought them to the group.

The first thing to know when contemplating people's needs in the context of social group work is that the concept does not connote *neediness*, nor does it intend to pathologize people with identified needs. A practitioner once shared a story about how her use of the word "needs" nearly got her fired. She was working in an organization that championed strength-based practices, but social group work was neither practiced nor understood. In fact, she was unsuccessful in exciting her colleagues about the possibilities of social group work for youth. One day in a meeting she noted the needs of youth in a particular program. When the meeting ended her boss turned to her and said, "If you ever use the word 'needs' again, I'll fire you." Thus did she come to understand that some folks interpret needs as a bad thing.

In truth, we human beings experience a range of needs; they may represent soaring ambitions and talents; the desire to be loved, to create, and to learn; to be a part of a community; or to fix something in one's life. We also share emotional, social, cognitive, developmental, and physical needs, to name the most prominent; and we all suffer burdens, losses, and challenges that amplify other needs. For example, we might need to build healthy relationships, give up drugs or alcohol, find a job, mourn the loss of a loved one, cope with divorce, or "come out" to family. Catastrophes, such as floods, earthquakes, and mass shootings can unite and meaningfully join people in common need. In the context of social group work, there is no shame or blame in the concept, recognition, and acceptance of human needs. If anything, a full and deep understanding of needs connotes an appreciation and respect for all that is human.

DOI: 10.4324/9781003002789-4

The skill of assessing need requires us to look fully and deeply at individuals and groups of individuals – to survey the landscape of human activity from an informed vantage point, drawing on knowledge, intuition, and experience. It is a skill and art form – art form because intuition (often polished by experience) is the X factor that can assist and inform an effective assessment. For example, you may observe that some children are actively engaged in activities, while others sit with heads down on the table or sit alone using their devices or wander about touching base with staff and peers. In such a situation, the trained group worker begins to infer and calculate needs. Now imagine a walk through a senior center. Some people seem isolated, some dance near the stage, and some sit in wheelchairs. What does the group worker think? Different population, similar apparent needs.

Assessing need also requires knowledge and understanding of human-development stages in order to help us to anticipate the kinds of needs that might exist in any given population or client group. Thus, the ability to identify needs (that might be met or well addressed in a group) constitutes a set of skills that requires not only the belief in the power of groups to help people but a multi-layered understanding of the ways in which that can happen. In short, your understanding of and belief in how groups can help people to meet their needs will propel your ability to make that happen and even further, to effectively gain support from administration for moving your ideas, vision, and process forward.

Major Concepts

Assessment
Context
Fit
Goodness of Fit
Membership/Belonging
Need
Perspective
Setting

Skills

Assess your work setting
Assess client perspective
Assess goodness of fit
Pay ongoing attention to need
Help people decide on membership

SKILL (NEED-BASED): ASSESS YOUR WORK SETTING

Elaboration: By *assess your work setting* we mean find out how the agency has tried to meet the needs of its client population through the use of groups.

Principle: Respect for context

Theory: Assessing your setting for group practice increases the likelihood of informed decisions.

Essay: There are many ways to gather information about your agency or work context. Talking with staff, clients, and management is one way. Another is to read organizational literature, such as manuals, mission statements, annual reports, and any other literature that describes the characteristics, norms, policies, and culture, and history (evolution) of your setting. Reading professional literature in

> **SKILL IN ACTION**
>
> With thoughts about forming a group for clients who seemed bored as they waited for lunch or their appointments, the worker wondered about group work at the center.
>
> *Has anyone done that here?* he wondered. *If so, how successfully? Are groups going on now? If so, what kinds? How did the past groups turn out? What are the current ones (if any) like? Who formed and worked or is working with them? Where did or do they meet? And what is or were their purposes? How have clients responded? Was the work supported by staff? Were/are the groups evaluated?*
>
> Armed with these questions and the likelihood of others as these got answered, the worker went to speak to as many people as he could about group work in this setting.

journals about settings like yours can provide a great deal of insight into what has been tried, what has succeeded (or not), and perhaps why or why not, what is within the scope of your context's mission, and what the community expects of your organization. What you want to avoid at all cost is to plan a group only to find out that one just like it was launched a few years back but quickly disbanded by the administration, or to have a new group be sabotaged by staff who might schedule individual sessions at the same time as your group meetings. So that your efforts to start a group are not in vain, it behooves you to explore and even dig a little to learn about the history of groups in your work setting in addition to what is happening there presently. You may even discover a history of successful groups that ended when the organization's sole group worker went on leave!

Assessing the work setting, which essentially refers to assessing the environment in which you practice or will practice, is always a useful and relevant skill. We do not work in a vacuum. We work in a system of some kind, and while systems usually do have a structure, they can also be a bit wiggly, shifting a little according to who is on the board, staff personalities, program or policy changes, or even slight changes in mission, for example. They can even change, as noted above, on such fickle variables as the loss of a staff member who undertook a certain type of activity, which then petered out when that person left!

Furthermore, systems have all sorts of needs that include first and foremost staying afloat financially, meeting mission mandates, and socio/political accountability. In short, the moral of this story is that *do not forget to consider organizational needs*! The organization needs action and services that fit and reflect its mission, and it also needs to meet certain legal, financial, and socio-political realities. Sometimes (although rare) those two categories of need will be in perfect sync with the needs that you see in your client groups, but sometimes they may not seem in such perfect sync; balancing (integrating whenever possible) organization and client needs is an important skill to develop.

SKILL (NEED-BASED): ASSESS CLIENT PERSPECTIVE

Elaboration: By *assess client perspective* we mean find out from the existing clients how they see their needs for service.

Principle: Respect for a person's voice

Theory: Knowledge of client needs lends direction to forming appropriate responses.

Essay: What your client needs (wants, wishes, desires) and what you think that person needs may be very different. Need or desires can be obfuscated or obscured by myriad factors including lack of insight (on the part of either party) a fragile sense of entitlement, or the fear of facing up to overwhelming needs, for example. Thus, your assessment of someone's needs goes hand in hand with that person's perception of need, and in making that assessment you should

> **SKILL IN ACTION**
>
> **Scenario 1.** *Jerry, I've learned that like you, most of the summer interns, are working on their own with few opportunities to engage with one another … What do you think about joining a group where interns could get together and share their experiences?*
>
> **Scenario 2.** *Mrs. Woods, I understand that you have many grandchildren. I'm wondering if you use all the new technology to stay in touch with them … Would you be interested in joining a group with others here to learn about using technology?*
>
> **Scenario 3.** *Paola, I've chatted with a lot of your classmates who are new immigrant students. Many feel homesick and lonely, much like what you've told me. What do you think about joining a group with other new immigrants to deal with some of these feelings and to make new friends?*

be direct and begin the process by asking people how they see their needs. To quote a fundamental social work precept: *start where the client is and work from there.*

Whether you are new to group work or a veteran professional, you are likely to reflexively see patterns of need that can be met by a group, patterns that generally include issues related to social interaction of one kind or other. Once that happens your task is to engage clients in conversations to test your hunch or perception against what they have to say. Here are three examples of doing just that.

- In your very large organization, you notice that summer interns are isolated in different programs. *Isolation* is the clue, here, and knowing what you know about being an intern, you postulate that they may be struggling, perhaps questioning their competence or wrestling with issues of protocol. You approach them individually to find out if your perceptions are correct. If so, perhaps an orientation group or ongoing support group for interns might be in order.
- At a senior center you chat with an octogenarian member who explains that she cannot navigate technology to chat with her grandchildren. You know that there are many clients in the center who might share that problem. In this scenario, *a need for human connection* is the clue, and you decide to explore this with others. If so, perhaps a task group to teach older adults the required technology for staying connected and even a set group time during which they might take advantage of the technology at the center is in order. Such a group would help

these folks to connect with families and additionally provide some connection among them based on a common need – a double bonanza!

- At a city high school over 50 students are new immigrants from the Dominican Republic. You have chatted with at least 20, most of whom are homesick and feel stressed about school. Several mentioned that they live with extended family members who they had never met before! In this case, the clues that group work might be in order are themes of *loss, loneliness*, and *adjustment struggles.* You imagine that these youth would like to feel/be less alone and have a stronger sense of belonging in their new world and wonder if a group to that end would help and what other needs might be relevant to starting up a group.

SKILL (NEED-BASED): ASSESS GOODNESS OF FIT

Elaboration: By *assess goodness of fit* we mean determine whether your idea for a group is in sync with what you have learned about existing needs.

Principle: Relevance of action

Theory: If goodness of fit exists between need and service, service is likely to be successful.

Essay: As you consider a group service and gather information from stakeholders, weigh the supports for it; be sure to consider the constraints or negative feedback and to explore where, how, and why you might encounter obstacles. If constraints or obstacles seem to outweigh support, you have a few choices. You can stick with your idea and explore and try to remove the obstacles. You can try to ignore the obstacles, hoping that over time they

---

SKILL IN ACTION

Reflecting on what each woman had been saying in counseling about coping with the loss of her husband, the worker thought,

The needs of these women seem to have a really good fit with group work.

What really stood out was the theme of feeling misunderstood. For example, she thought,

Angie would like to be with people who get what she's going through. Camille's tired of well-meaning but unhelpful advice. Sofia could use some support to breathe and not feel obligated to "just move forward." Jackie said that she uses a lot of energy to hide her grief so as to not "bother" others ...

I think that my idea of some kind of support group for coping with loss is on the right track here ... I'm going to check it out with each of them.

---

will dissipate. You can try to win over potential or likely saboteurs. Or you can rethink your idea, move back a few steps in the planning process, and start talking with stakeholders about a modified or changed plan.

If at any point you find yourself trying to sell the idea of the group, take that as a red flag – a signal to step back, listen carefully to the client or stakeholder, and to take seriously any obstacles or objections to the group. By selling the group the worker is putting pressure on potential candidates or colleagues, trying to convince them that the group will be a good thing. It evokes the dubious adage of *trust me*. People will often yield to pressure in the moment but once away from that pressure are likely to retreat to their original position. In other words, you might be able to convince people in the moment to agree to attend a first session, but do not be surprised if they do not show up. That is human nature: many of us will feign interest to please a person in power, to avoid conflict, or to escape a conversation. Stay in tune with that possibility.

In sum, when you consider all the issues involved in forming a group, you are not trying to figure out how to sell a product. Rather, you engage in an open, honest, and dynamic process of determining goodness of fit between any needs you learn about and any ideas that are forming in your head. In that process you explore both positive responses and objections in order to acquire vital feedback. Information obtained from authentic conversations with clients, colleagues, and stakeholders is pure gold. Consider feedback as data and ponder the data – all of it whether it pleases you or not – with appreciation for its ability to steer you in the right direction.

Differential Application: Assessing goodness of fit is a skill that applies any time you are trying to figure out if two ideas mesh well together. For example, you assess goodness of fit between a potential group member's goals and the purpose of a group you have in mind when you evaluate whether the group you have in mind will meet that person's needs. You also assess goodness of fit between the mission of an organization and your personal needs and goals when you consider whether to accept a job offer. We believe that this concept of differential application applies broadly enough to move this narrative beyond a few examples and thus, we offer you the list below of the many and varied ways in which this skill may be applied.

1 Goodness of fit between the idea for a group and the nature of your work setting.
2 Goodness of fit between your idea for a group and needs of potential group members as identified first and foremost by them and secondarily, by the agency.
3 Goodness of fit between identified need and a potential group purpose.
4 Goodness of fit between what a client wants and what the group can offer.
5 Goodness of fit between group purpose and a group activity.
6 Goodness of fit between group activity and stage of group development.
7 Goodness of fit between group development and nature of intervention.
8 Goodness of fit between choice of intervention and the intent you have in mind.
9 Goodness of fit between intent (objectives) and outcomes.
10 Goodness of fit between group outcome and group purpose.
11 Goodness of fit between group purpose and organizational context (mission).

SKILL (NEED-BASED): PAY ONGOING ATTENTION TO NEED

Elaboration: By *pay ongoing attention to need* we mean identify what needs or desires exist at any given moment.

Principle: Awareness of the dynamic nature of need

Theory: Remaining attuned to needs gives you the information required to take relevant action.

Essay: If you pay attention to what people say they need or want and base your idea for a group service on that, you are more likely to have an outcome that is meaningful to the people in the group, i.e., relevant to participants.

The skill of assessing need is employed prominently in planning and starting up a group. Its utility extends into each stage of group

---

SKILL IN ACTION

Reflecting on the previous session the worker recalled Mrs. K's personal revelations and wondered about its impact on others.

Each woman seems to be really invested in the group … You can sense it in how much they are sharing their stories, especially when they talk about their guilt and frustration as parents.

The worker tuned into the notion that each member's needs for support might change over time, however, as they responded to one another's feelings and deep insecurities.

I wonder if and how their needs might change as their talk becomes deeper. Will the group need more direct support from me as they traverse areas of increased vulnerability?

---

development as the worker observes and assesses the changing needs of individual members and the group as a whole over time. Needs are dynamic, ever present, evolving, changing, and demanding. For example, the weekly support group highlighted in the sidebar recruited parents whose children showed disruptive and aggressive behavior in school. The group's stated purpose was to help members to manage their children's behavior. During the course of that group, however, needs evolved and changed as members explored the meaning of the group purpose. For example, in the early stage of group life Mrs. K. expressed frustration with the teacher and school dean for "non-stop complaint calls" about her son. Her co-members shared similar frustrations. Many sessions later Mrs. K. divulged that she was always angry with her son for causing so many problems at school and at home, and later, down the road, she admitted that she felt like she had caused her son's problems.

Can you see how the needs of this member seem to have shifted over time? At the start of the group it appeared that the collective need was for support to deal with their children's disruptive behavior. As the group evolved it began to look a little more like the need was for support in dealing with guilty feelings about having perhaps contributed to that behavior. In this scenario the worker first assessed group members' needs as individuals in order to plan a group, then as members of a new group with certain stated needs around which they initially convened, and then later as members of the more mature group who may require yet other kinds of support from one another and from the worker. This is what is meant by paying attention to *ongoing* needs – staying in touch with the nuances of group process such that when it may need a shift in focus, the worker is both sensitive and open to that possibility and responds with a commensurate shift in attention, often consisting of a question to the group asking if a new and significant need is being expressed.

Following the parent group session in which this particular member talked about regrets and guilt, the worker reflected on the impact of personal revelations on other members. She reflected on each person and the evolution of that person's investment in the group as sharing became increasingly intimate. She tuned into the notion that each member's need for support might change as they responded to and tolerated the sharing of some deeply held insecurities. Finally, she wondered how many might share similar feelings at some point and how as a result, their needs might continue to change with increased authenticity and depth. She asked herself, *Will the group as a whole require more direct support as members become increasingly vulnerable?*

The worker's recognition of changing needs in this instance is central to her role in the group. She had observed over time that as parents faced their own doubts and failings, they began to normalize their experiences, forgive themselves for perceived wrongdoings, and take more responsibility for meeting the purpose of the group, i.e., to better manage their children's behavior. Ultimately, group process revealed group members' differing needs in the kinds of help and support needed to that end. For example, one member recognized that her child might benefit from an evaluation as school personnel had suggested and acknowledged the importance of better understanding his behavior. Another acknowledged that she needed help in setting limits and following through on consequences, and yet another realized that her son captured the family's attention with trouble at school but received limited recognition for good behavior. Thus, while the overall purpose of the group remained relevant, over time parents identified the specific relevance of that purpose to their unique situation and went to work on the tasks that would help them each to reach their goals.

SKILL (NEED-BASED): HELP PEOPLE DECIDE ON MEMBERSHIP

Elaboration: By *help people decide on membership* we mean help individuals to decide if the group being formed is right for them.

Principle: Self-determination

Theory: Inviting self-determination from the start reinforces people's right to have a say.

Essay: Inviting clients to decide on membership means to ask them to reflect on whether or not there is a good fit between their needs (and wants), and the group (group purpose) on which you ultimately land. Asking potential members to make this kind of decision accomplishes several important goals. First, it begins to set into motion the goal of promoting self-determination (Bernstein 1962) by asking people to contribute to their

---

SKILL IN ACTION

Jinelle, you seem to have mixed feelings about joining the group I just described. You think you could help others, but; what is the "but" about? (Jinelle says that she may not be able to share her situation.)

Mmm, you talked the other day about your anger and problems with bosses; might you get help with that in a group? (Jinelle shakes her head no.)

Okay, I respect your feelings. What if I said everyone struggles over sharing stories to begin with, so you wouldn't be alone … and that things would move slowly to keep everyone comfortable. Would that help? (Jinelle repeats her reluctance.)

Well, this may not be the right time for you to join a group or maybe not the group for you. Tell you what; if you change your mind, let me know? And thanks for talking straight with me; I appreciate it.

---

destiny – in this case, with regard to group membership (Falck 1989). *Does the group we have in mind appeal to them? If so, how? If not, why not? Do they see themselves participating in such a group? If so, how? If not, why not? Do they believe that they could make good use of the group? If so, how so? And if not, why not?*

Asking potential group members to provide feedback on your idea for a group with these and other such questions helps to ensure that your efforts will not be in vain, because you will have received valuable feedback about those efforts. This feedback provides the building blocks for "getting it right" – that is, for ultimately landing on a purpose that is meaningful and relevant to those whose needs your service is trying to meet. Inviting potential members to decide on membership also sets the stage for your relationship with them as one in which they are invited to have a real voice in sharing control over their destinies, not in just identifying their needs or problems (Falck 1989). It also begins the journey to strength-centered practice by recognizing and acknowledging members-to-be as being significant in shaping the group (Lietz 2007). Even further, it helps potential members to understand your role as a person of *service*. In other words, your desire for their opinion helps them to begin to see that you see your role as one of helping them to meet their needs, not one of imposing your own ideas of what should or should not be. They see this in the sincerity of your questions asking them what they think about what you think.

Of course, by the time you are finally recruiting members, you may feel highly invested in your idea. You have worked hard, checking in with various stakeholders, listening carefully, and incorporating feedback. You have met with staff and inquired about constraints and obstacles. You have talked with many clients about your ideas and taken into account their views as you ultimately landed on a group purpose that would cover the goals you heard, and you have even thought about which types of content (talking, activity, task, etc.) might make sense. Now, you are at the point of inviting people to join the group. How tempting it is to tell people that they must join because the group is tailor-made for them! When we care about people, we so much want what we think is good for them and have a difficult time letting go of our own ideas. Have you ever had a piece of cake so delicious to you that you tried to force it on someone else even when they keep telling you that they do not like that flavor? *Try it*, you say; *I promise that you'll love it*! Mmm … you may feel similarly about inviting people into a group you have spent so much time thinking about, planning, and for which you have made all sorts of arrangements.

What is important to remember is that your responsibility now is to help potential group members to consider carefully whether the group as you have presented it has a goodness of fit with their needs *as they see them*. If they express ambivalence or say no, your responsibility is not to convince them or "sell" them anything but rather to acknowledge the ambivalence or the declination. … You can certainly ask to hear a little bit more in case their concern is something that you can resolve or clarify. However, and most importantly, they may be right; the group as you have conceptualized it may not be a good fit with what they want at that time. Finally, it is important to remember that even if you hear some workers talk about whether people are right for a group, the issue is really whether a group is right for what a person needs or wants. Maintaining this mindset will help to tailor services appropriately while preventing judgment on the "rightness" or "suitability" of people.

To summarize, when you talk with potential group members about joining a group you have in mind, absolutely do explore their reasoning. In fact, asking them to talk about why they believe the group would be a good fit is just as important and informative as asking them why they believe that it would not be. Whichever direction the conversation takes, do not label a declination as a form of resistance (and thus try to brow beat that resistance away). Your task is to help them to make the best decision *as they ultimately see it at that moment*.

A very few exceptions notwithstanding (as in mandated groups) people have a right to say no. In fact, increasing attention to the rights of consumerism has gained momentum over the last two or three decades, and as a result human service has started to be more interested in consumer evaluation. That said, the field is still very inconsistent in asking people we call clients what they think of us, but doing just that – asking potential group members what they think of what we think – opens the door to a relationship that recognizes the "service" component of social service that will be relevant to needs and desires.

Unit 3:2 Skill Set
Purpose

Overview

Social service practice should be purposeful. In fact, being purposeful is a hallmark that separates the professional from the technician (along with a body of ethical conduct and a theoretical base). If we understand the "why" of what we do, we can repeat it – we can do what we do on purpose rather than haphazardly. When we are asked why we selected a particular group purpose, we can articulate the "why" of the group we are forming; being purposeful helps to prevent us from constantly figuring out what to do and why. The concept of purpose plays an enormous role in social group work practice, helping the worker to articulate the logic and thus relevance of any given action from planning a group (why such a group would be appropriate in a certain context) to the length of a group (e.g., why it makes sense for the group to meet semi-weekly over three months).

The set of skills related to purpose reflects an enormous range of attention to this concept, from thinking about what kind of group purpose might make sense given the needs you see at work to thinking about how best to operationalize (put into action) a purpose with a group to thinking "purpose" even when you are not in a meeting. Think of group purpose as the umbrella under which various individual goals – those particular goals of group members – logically and reasonably fall. Although we form groups around common needs, individual needs are almost always a little bit different, and it is a group's purpose that will bind those needs (and thus group members) together. For example, in a support group to help members cope with breast cancer, one member states that she needs help to cope with her husband's indifference. Another member whose mother died of breast cancer wants to reduce her anxiety. A third member feels "untethered" with a constant foreboding that "the other shoe is about to fall," while yet another has withdrawn from friends, is unable to engage in a social life, and wants to get back to "some kind of normal." All of these women identify needs connected to their cancers, the common thread that binds them, but have different personal goals. Helping the group to assist each member to reach her goal while assisting the group as a whole to reach its overarching purpose (to help them to meet each of those goals), is the dual task of the worker.

In a different example, eight middle-school boys join a group with the following stated purpose: to help members to act and think like chess masters. Every member wants to learn to play chess, and with help from the worker and other members each one has identified personally meaningful goals. Their goals do not focus on learning about the rules and strategies of chess (that is a shared objective for all), but the worker

DOI: 10.4324/9781003002789-5

engages each of them to identify a behavior or mindset that could improve their game. Two members want to learn to control their tempers, especially when they lose a game. Two others want to play less impulsively (*I want to think carefully before I make a move, because I always think of a better move a second after I put my piece down, and it's really aggravating*). Another member wants to be "level-headed." Yet another wants to stop "ranking" on his opponents (*No one wants to play with me anymore*), and the last member of the group thinks that he needs to focus better on listening to the rules and feedback (*I drift a lot ...*). Two also want to try harder, to not give up so easily. The worker, who had thought a great deal about the group purpose and recognized that there is much more to the game than rules and strategies, had explored this line of reasoning in recruiting each boy and also when the group started, so that the boys were aware of one another's personal goals and thus able to help one another with those goals as when the group formed, and they engaged in chess.

Finally, a group's purpose should be stated so simply that everyone involved can repeat the group-purpose statement at will without looking at a piece of paper. Getting a statement of purpose to that point, however, is almost always easier said than done, because group purpose reflects the why of a group – why these people at this time are joining in common cause to address a particular topic. Group purpose does not reflect what a group is going to do, which is generally what people new to the work tend to say (as in, *the group will talk about ...*). What a group will do reflects *content* (the what of group process), not purpose (the why of being together).

A good way to begin a statement of purpose is to begin with these words; *The purpose of the group is to help members to ...* (go ahead and finish the statement with some groups you have in mind; remember, the statement needs to be an articulation of your offer to help those who will collaborate together to accomplish something to which they all relate).

Major Concepts

> Goal vs. content
> Group purpose
> Membership
> Operationalization
> Purpose
> Purpose as a fluid dynamic
> Purpose as a need-driven dynamic
> The why of something

Skills

> Conceptualize a potential group purpose
> Try it* on for size (*your idea about a group purpose)
> Land on a particular group purpose
> Operationalize group purpose
> Consider size of membership in relation to group purpose
> Pay ongoing attention to group purpose
> Constantly think "purpose"

SKILL (PURPOSE-BASED): CONCEPTUALIZE
A POTENTIAL GROUP PURPOSE

Elaboration: By *conceptualize a potential group purpose* we mean consider one or more purposes around which you might form a group based on identified needs.

Principle: Relevance of action

Theory: A correctly conceptualized purpose responds to identified needs.

Essay: In social group work practice identified needs and desires drive purpose. That is, in considering the possibility of group service, it is your clients' needs that will drive your thinking and your ultimate decision about a group's purpose (why the group is being formed). Said conversely, whatever group purpose you consider should be based on the needs and wants that you have identified from speaking with

> **SKILL IN ACTION**
>
> With a list of vets from his supervisor and her request to *get these guys back on their feet,* the worker called the men to talk about challenges in returning stateside and interest in forming a group around those challenges. The vets noted employment, marital discord, rage, and insomnia.
>
> *The men do seem interested in a group, but they are reluctant to get into anything like therapy ... On the other hand, they did all talk about feeling lost. I wonder if a group purpose formed around one foot in Afghanistan and one foot at home might work. A purpose related to that theme would be broad enough to cover all the ways in which the men could try to build a bridge home while allowing that bridge-building to look a little different for each of them.*

potential members and agency staff (with the needs identified by your clients prioritized). This means that everything about the nature of a potential group purpose is determined by the needs you note, i.e., which types of individual goals fit under the umbrella of a particular purpose, how long it would take to reasonably achieve such a purpose, and the extent to which such a purpose would fit within your agency's mission.

While those needs come predominantly from your client population, the concept of need (see need-based skill set) also pertains to those of the agency, such as what it needs to meet its mission. Thus, a group purpose should remain within its parameters, unless of course your administration has determined that it is time for something new. Then, you have a whole new set of parameters but ones that are approved by Management.

A group purpose, as noted in the Introduction, reflects the "why" of a group. This means that it is not about what the group will do (talk, activity, perform, etc.) or how the group will do it (its actual process) but rather, why it is logical for these people at this time to come together for a collective service (however defined and including recreation and education as well as clinical service). Thus, a group purpose statement is usually short and sweet. Here are some examples along with examples of how the varied goals of individual members might fall under that umbrella statement:

Group Purpose Statement Example 1: *The purpose of this group is to help these children to do better in school.* Jane has very poor study habits; the group can help her to develop better study habits. John is too shy to speak up in class; the group can help him to build his self-confidence. Jose is socially isolated with few friends, making it difficult for him to focus on his work; over the time, the group can produce new friends for Jose. Jenny gets frustrated easily and stops trying; the group can encourage her to stick with it. Victoria is a perfectionist and takes too long to get anything finished; the group can help her to live with "good enough." Thus, in this group all the members are having trouble in school for various reasons, but they all fit under an umbrella goal (purpose) of "doing better in school." The beauty of their differences is that each one can help the others with ideas precisely because what they need and what they have to offer one another in the form of ideas, tips, suggestions, and support is different as well.

Group Purpose Statement Example 2: *The purpose of this group is to provide these recently widowed men a place to socialize with like others.* Each of the men in this group has suffered the loss of a lifetime partner and given all we know about such loss could benefit from structured time with others who generally know how they feel. The content of the group might be to talk, to reminisce, to share how they are grieving, and perhaps strategies they are using to help comfort themselves, but it might also be an activity. For example, one such group was formed around weekly two-hour sessions in which members learned how to cook healthy and satisfying meals for themselves. The session included cooking and eating with shopping and planning homework, some of which required them to be in contact between sessions, enhancing opportunities to connect and socialize.

Group Purpose Statement Example 3: *The purpose of this group is to help these seventh graders to cope with the loss of a loved one.* Sam's mother died in an accident at work; he wished he had hugged her goodbye that morning. Jade's grandmother who raised her died from cancer; Jade wondered if the stress of dealing with Jade's school problems had caused the cancer. Denali's mother and five-year-old sister died in a fire; Denali wondered if he could have prevented the fire by coming directly home from school. Christian's favorite uncle died from a drug overdose; Christian knew that his uncle had used drugs and wondered if he could have helped more. Ileana's grandmother died in her sleep; Ileana felt grief-stricken that she never said goodbye. Shawana's father died in a car accident right after they had argued; Shawana blamed herself. The worker recognized two key factors in common: the self-blame that all the children were experiencing and the fact that developmentally, early adolescents are reluctant to ever stand out in the crowd, making the death of a loved especially difficult to navigate. In their bereavement group the children felt relief as they learned that others shared their reactions and feelings; the shared purpose of the group bound them together. Further, they were not "crazy" or weird; they were in grief, and the moment that they recognized their feelings of loss as normal, they felt an epiphany, a tremendous relief.

SKILL (PURPOSE-BASED): TRY IT* ON FOR SIZE
(*YOUR IDEA ABOUT A GROUP PURPOSE)

Elaboration: By *try it on for size* we mean share your idea/s for a potential group purpose with all stakeholders in order to discern desirability and feasibility.

Principle: Contextualized action

Theory: Feedback on ideas helps the worker to select an option for action that fits the bill.

Essay: In using this skill the worker considers potential members' *significant others*, i.e., individuals related to those who are interested in the group you have in mind. For example, it might be wise or at least useful to seek the approval of the parents related to children for whom you have a particular group in mind. Use appropriate language adapted to each type of stakeholder. Talking to children about your ideas would use different language than would a conversation with parents or agency administration, for example. Talking with members of administration might include references to such factors as quantity and/or quality of service, reduction of recidivism, and alignment of your ideas with agency mission or community expectations, while talking to children would probably include in very simple language what's "in it" for them to participate, as you see it. If all relevant parties end up liking your idea, your chance of a successful group experience increases exponentially.

When you test out your ideas with other relevant persons, you need to be prepared for input! In short, you may need to tweak or even redirect altogether what you thought was a good idea. Be prepared, keep an open mind, and listen very carefully to what others have to say. Many if not most groups end up being a hybrid of what the worker thought to begin with, what clients thought, and what the agency thought (or would accept). Even further, be prepared to "size down" your idea. Some group purposes are much too broad for the time that an agency can offer, for example, so be prepared to chisel a little off on an original idea into one that is feasible, desirable, realistic, and workable from every point of view. A group may not be able to improve the range of parenting skills, for example, but it may be able to focus on a particular aspect of parenting, such as setting limits or providing structure or helping children to better manage their time. It is not a sign of failure to begin with a "grand" idea and to end up with a smaller yet workable piece of that idea that does in fact provide people with real, valuable, and concrete help.

SKILL IN ACTION

On the phone with the mother of a middle-aged woman with schizophrenia.

I'd like to hear what you think about my idea for a group, and I'm counting on your frankness. .... What do you think of a group for parents who need to make plans for their adult children's care? I've learned from you and others how hard it is – complex to plan and find resources and also that the idea of separation is heartbreaking ...

Here's my idea ... I wonder if a group to help you find some peace of mind in all of this could be useful.

Everyone in the group would have a lot in common and could support each other. You could help each other too, because you all have experience and information to share.

Your thoughts?

SKILL (PURPOSE-BASED): LAND ON A PARTICULAR GROUP PURPOSE

Elaboration: By *land on a particular group purpose*, we mean make a decision with relevant others about the group to be.

Principle: Inclusion of interested parties

Theory: Involving stakeholders in decision making creates collective ownership of that decision.

Essay: To land on a particular group purpose means to actually make a decision about which group purpose that you go with, if you will. You may have had a few ideas to begin with, but at some point, it will become clear which one is the most desirable to your clients and the most feasible in your setting. The process begins by having conversations with relevant others, as noted above, about the idea that is starting to make most sense to you; continues by seeking consensus from

> **SKILL IN ACTION**
>
> Social worker musing about the purpose of reproductive health groups for teens.
>
> *The young people said that they need more information about the mechanics of sex. But given their age, they also need support to understand it and especially around relationships and values .... A few group ideas there ....*
>
> *Now, the funders of this grant want to help youth avoid pregnancy though their approach would be to just say no. Mmm .... Also, so many young people are having sex, so this is also a safety issue. Perhaps safety, voice, and values are the three key elements.*
>
> Ultimately and all things considered, the worker landed on a theme of helping young people to make good decisions about their sexual health.
>
> *It means different things to different people ... which is exactly what a purpose should allow for.*

all those others (and being open to possible tweaks); and ends with a collective commitment to one idea. It is important for all stakeholders to be a part of the decision-making process here, because when people exercise authority over decisions that affect them, they are more committed to those decisions. This includes clients who will be in the group, staff that will be asked to support your efforts, and administrators who will be expected to sanction your work.

People new to group work often worry about landing on a particular group purpose, because in essence it means giving up a number of possibilities for service, all of which are usually worthwhile. Service needs to be delivered in context, however, meaning in this case that it needs to be realistic (Steinberg 2014a). There is perhaps no bigger set-up for failure than to have a group purpose that is so grandiose that no group could ever achieve it (as in, *This group will alleviate members' depression*). Equally problematic is a purpose that is so broad that no one really understands it (as in, *This rap group will be for you whatever you want it to be*)! In the first instance, better to identify a small piece of that dynamic, such as a particular concrete issue (e.g., medication management) or behavior (e.g., getting through a day) or need (e.g., caring for a family) that a group might focus on and help its members with. In the second, a "whatever" purpose offers nothing concrete to bind members to one another (as in, *We seem to want to "rap" about different things ...*) or to the group as a system of service (as in, *Why are we here again?*). Furthermore, the first instance leaves the worker to navigate an array of interventions, none of them

> **Note**
>
> Casework in a group (Kurland & Salmon 1992) refers to a process in which the worker offers individual attention to one member at a time. It has also been referred to as the aggregate therapy of individuals (Hartford 1971). In this instance group members have little if anything to do with one another except sit in a common circle. The main character of the play is the worker, who takes center stage and remains as be-all and end-all of the helping process. Why would such a group ever be formed? As one social group worker once was heard to say, it makes good c-e-n-t-s to serve people all at once even if it does not make good s-e-n-s-e to ignore what group members could bring to one another if the worker would only get out of the way.

truly fitting the bill for collective use but rather, leading to what has been referred to by some scholars as *casework in a group* (Kurland & Salmon 1992), while in the second scenario there is no really good answer if group members keep having to ask the question, *Why are we here?* Were a group to be ongoing in a forever kind of way, it might in fact be able to tackle an enormous purpose, but this is not usually the case. Thus, a group will be more successful if its purpose is tangible enough for all members (1) to be able to articulate and repeat without looking at the statement on paper because each person understands it clearly; (2) to understand its personal relevance; (3) to be able to work toward it and know whether in fact progress is being made; and (4) to actually achieve it.

SKILL (PURPOSE-BASED): OPERATIONALIZE GROUP PURPOSE

Elaboration: By *operationalize group purpose* we mean engage in the kind of planning for a group that will result in a specific time and place that satisfies all contingencies.

Principle: Action in context

Theory: An idea well planned sets a solid foundation for action.

Essay: A good idea for action needs to consider a number of factors or details about how to execute that idea or said otherwise, how to translate the idea into real action. In working with groups there is a great deal to be done, as you have already read, from the moment you enter a context in which you wonder if a group service might be warranted to actually sitting for the very first time with a group of people you call clients (or perhaps staff or significant others) in order to launch the first meeting.

SKILL IN ACTION

The worker landed on a group purpose: *to help foster care workers better cope with job stress.*

Meeting with her boss to discuss structure, she said that she hoped to meet on every other Friday for 8 weeks from 3:30 to 5:00. *That works for everyone who is joining. Supervisors*, she adds, *have agreed to cover drop-ins and calls.*

Still, we need a private space, so we aren't interrupted. What about the boardroom?

It's a good set up; we can move chairs. Is it always empty at that time on Friday?

Also, is food allowed in that room? I want to offer refreshments.

Oh, and we'll have a wheelchair-bound member. Is that room accessible? I haven't seen it in a long time. And is a nearby bathroom accessible?

Operationalizing a group purpose begins with the process you have already undertaken: speaking with relevant others and landing on one particular purpose. It also includes many questions to ask, all within the context of group purpose. Some questions are conceptual (e.g., *Given its purpose, how often should this type of group meet?*); and some are concrete or temporal (e.g., *Given agency policies, can this group meet its purpose within time-related and other constraints?*). This means that you will need to reflect on the "why" of any direction you ponder. For example, why should the group you have in mind meet weekly, or why should it meet for two hours at a time? Again, your responses may be conceptual (based on the nature or intensity of need, for example) or concrete (in a school, for example, 45-minute class periods). In short, to operationalize a group purpose means to translate your selected group purpose into action that will set a solid foundation on which to begin.

SKILL (PURPOSE-BASED): CONSIDER SIZE OF MEMBERSHIP IN RELATION TO GROUP PURPOSE

Elaboration: By *consider size of membership in relation to group purpose,* we mean consider how much time and space each member is likely to need in order to use the group effectively.

Principle: Respect for high-quality work

Theory: Making sure that the group is not too large for everyone to participate in a meaningful way ensures that process can move beyond the superficial.

Essay: The number of members in a group is an important element to consider when thinking about purpose. The equation goes something like this: A group should be large enough to provide enough voices to stimulate its process without being so large as to be chaotic. How this relates to group purpose is as follows. To a large extent the group's purpose will dictate an appropriate size of membership. If a purpose requires in-depth talking on the part of each member, then each meeting must provide enough time for each voice to be heard in a meaningful way. If a purpose requires activity other than talking, then each meeting must provide enough time for each member to engage in that activity in a personal and interpersonal way.

Contemplating the degree to which a group can meet its purpose given its size is a basic way of showing respect for both those who participate and for the group service itself. For example, a group that is large in size but short on time will permit only token interaction (thus, not very respectful of members), creating a forum for what is often called "lip service," (showing disrespect for the nature and potential of groups as a meaningful service medium). In contrast, a group of three, which dwindles down to one or two with absences will have a difficult time remaining both stimulated and stimulating. Neither of these scenarios will help move the process toward meeting a group purpose. This is not to say that some help cannot take place, but in the former case it is likely to be, as noted, superficial (and thus frustrating for many) and in the latter case, although help can take place even between two remaining members or even one member and the worker, the whole concept of *group* work becomes moot. For example, psycho-educational groups, the purpose of which is to impart information, generally offer little opportunity for participants to fully integrate and personally apply that information. Attendees may ask a question or two here and

---

SKILL IN ACTION

We're under pressure to hit high numbers, the worker mused to herself, *but the clients who like this idea hope to talk about their lives and challenges as caregivers ....*

With 90 minutes what is a good group size? These folks feel isolated and even have lost a sense of who they are beyond their caregiver role... The last thing they need is to feel obsolete in a large group or not have time to really share their feelings.

I know we are under pressure about numbers, but going past 8 – already big for a group in which we hope for intimacy – won't work. With 8, if 1or 2 group members are missing we still have 6, enough for good conversation.

If I'm asked why not more, I'll talk about all the issues that these folks have raised and how they need time to be addressed with meaning. I wonder if I might form 2 groups ....

there, but the opportunity for in-depth dialogue around the meaning and significance of what they hear is generally lost. At the other extreme, as noted just above, having only one or two members present not only renders the concept of groupness moot but undermines the very nature of group work by ignoring the value of input from several voices.

SKILL (PURPOSE-BASED): PAY ONGOING ATTENTION TO GROUP PURPOSE

Elaboration: By *pay ongoing attention to group purpose*, we mean check in frequently with members about the continued desirability and applicability of the group purpose.

Principle: Relevance

Theory: Including stakeholders in ongoing confirmation that a purpose is appropriate ensures that direction remains on target.

Essay: It would be comforting to think that once we settle or "land" on a group purpose we are home free. The truth is, group purpose is not static. It is dynamic, a little wiggly, and requires ongoing surveillance in order to ensure that if members' needs change, the purpose is modified to accommodate that change. Of course,

---

SKILL IN ACTION

To the group: *You know how important a group purpose is by now; we've been talking about it a lot!*

But guess what? (chuckling) *We're not done! We'll talk about it a lot more! For example, if I'm not 100% clear, I'll ask how what you just said relates to our purpose. You might even get frustrated with me! And in fact, everyone here has the same right. Not clear? Not sure about the work at hand? Chime in and ask how the moment relates to our purpose.*

And … even beyond that, just so you know, I'll check in often to make sure that our purpose still suits you. Sometimes a group purpose gets changed over time, so it's very important that we keep an eye on it to make sure we're always on track and on target as you all see it.

---

tweaking or redirecting a group's purpose is less likely for a very short-term group than for a long-term group. Still, the key to effective service of any kind is relevance; thus, it is essential to constantly confirm and reconfirm that the purpose selected is relevant as the group moves along in the event that members' needs (or wants) do change. Sometimes a new need emerges that members feel supersede the need that originally brought them together; in long-term groups that original need might well be met but members would like to stay together to meet other common needs. Whatever the reason, good practice means being vigilant that group purpose remains relevant.

Reviewing a group's purpose on an ongoing basis can be as simple as asking a member at each meeting to articulate the purpose as it has been identified and is currently understood (e.g., *Who can say what our purpose is as we think we understand it today?*) and seeking a renewal of commitment to that purpose for the work of the meeting (e.g., *Are we still on this page and good to go for today?*). It can be also reviewed at the end of each meeting in the context of evaluating how well the work of the day spoke to the group's purpose as understood by all participants. Both of these ways of reviewing a group's purpose will allow ongoing affirmation or if need be, some slight tweaking of process or purpose in order to make sure that content remains relevant, significant, and useful.

SKILL (PURPOSE-BASED): CONSTANTLY THINK PURPOSE

Elaboration: By *constantly "think purpose"* we mean reflect at all times on the relationship between needs of the moment and the purpose of your proposed (or actual) action.

Principle: Keeping actions in sync with goals

Theory: Identifying the purpose of an action keeps that action in clear sight of its relevance.

Essay: This skill of "thinking purpose" does not only apply to what we say and do in a group meeting, it applies to everything that we say or do with regard to the group. Truth be told, "think purpose" is a directive that does or at least should apply to all aspects of practice. The fundamental question for the worker is this:

SKILL IN ACTION

Scanning as three teens join the group late, which stops the talking. *Welcome Pedro, April, Aidan; glad you made it!*

Thinking quickly. *These three seem invested when they're here, but it's the 3rd week they are late. I wonder if they're aware of the impact of the lateness …. I think we need to talk about this. If our purpose is to help kids build healthy peer relations, then being aware of "other" is key … so even if there is a good reason, we need to talk about it.*

To the group: *Okay, I'm glad you're all here, but let's hold the conversation for a bit. This is the 3rd week that Pedro, April, and Aidan are 20 minutes late. We need to talk about how it's affecting all of us.*

Can we start by finding out what's causing the lateness so often?

What purpose will/would it serve for me to say/do X or Y? Asking yourself this question whenever you are thinking of taking any kind of action in practice will help you to keep your actions both logical and relevant.

Even reflecting on how appropriate it would be to disclose any personal information about yourself can benefit from asking yourself what the purpose of doing so would be; would it help or hinder your practice? For example, would it move a group's work forward? If so, how? If not, why not? In either case, understanding the purpose of disclosing or not serves as a very concrete and stable framework for making your decision (see Appendix C on self-disclosure).

Another example might be whether or not to interject your thoughts into a group conversation. Would doing so help to move the group's work forward or not? Would doing so meet a need that you note in (or that is directly expressed by) the group at this moment? Perhaps it would actually stifle the group, because members might be concerned about not sharing your viewpoint, for example, or perhaps it would stimulate the group, which has been very quiet and could use a bit of prodding. The issue for practice is to understand what purpose speaking at this moment would achieve, once again serving as a framework for making your decision about the value of your two cents' worth. This very simple question you ask of yourself is a very direct way of keeping yourself honest, helping you to identify why you should or should not say or do something. Would it serve the needs of the moment? Or might it serve only your needs (as in making you, the worker, feel good in some way or other)?

Thus, to return to the point made in Part 1 about skills being behaviors we know, constantly thinking "purpose" is simply a professional way to follow the adage, *think before you speak*. It just adds the small element of exploring why you might or might not say or do what you have in mind so that what you decide is helpful (moves things along in a positive way) rather than harmful (inadvertently frightens or stifles altogether).

Unit 3:3 Skill Set
Worker Role

Overview

People who work with groups normally do so according to some theoretical framework, often creating practices that may look quite different from one another. A medical-model practice, for example, tends to place and keep the professional at the center of all things, in the role of expert in all areas of potential help ranging from identifying member needs (why form a group in the first place) to desirable outcomes (what members' goals should be). The worker in this model also holds all the reins so that, for example and to mix metaphors, the worker is at the center of a wheel with all spokes to members going to and from the worker but without any definitive spokes running between and among all the members. This often leads to what social group work method has coined as *casework in a group* (Kurland & Salmon 1992) or the *aggregate therapy of individuals* (Hartford 1971), both of which have been presented in earlier discussions.

In this book and in rather dramatic contrast to that model, we propose the worker as one expert among many, the presumption being that people are generally expert in their own lives and in addition almost always have insights to offer others (Schwartz 2005). In this model, called the social group work model (Breton 2006; Middleman 1978; Middleman & Wood 1990a; Papell & Rothman 1966), the worker's role is to bring a particular expertise in catalyzing useful and helpful group process through which participants use their own strengths (skills and talents, both concrete and conceptual) to help one another to achieve goals that they have identified and agree to (Breton 2006; Cohen & Olshever 2013; Lietz 2007; Galinsky & Schopler 1971; Kurland & Salmon 1990; Lee 2001).

Thus, in effect, we see the group worker primarily as educator, devoted to educating members about desirable ways of acting and interacting in the group. The worker's role is not to present a blank slate; rather, the worker brings a clear and explicit vision of the ways in which group members should relate to one another. Everyone in the group has ideas about how to meet the needs and desires that brought them to this group at this time. Your job as the worker is not to be an expert in what brought people to the group, since it is impossible to be an expert in all things for all people, but to help them to help one another to meet those needs and desires. In short, it is to set in motion certain ways of interrelating (norms) by describing their benefits (values). All people have some strengths (skills and talents) to use on their own behalf and to lend others including, for example, a homeless person's ability to survive in a harsh world or to help someone else to do so. Thus, your primary contribution is

DOI: 10.4324/9781003002789-6

an understanding of and ability to catalyze that process in order to fully harness those strengths; hence the benefit of education and training in the method (Steinberg 2014a; see also skill set for *mutual aid*, pp. 80–90).

The skills in this section, *Worker Role*, all aim to help the worker to conduct practice to that end – to set up a group and to intervene in group process in ways that constantly identify and harness the skills and talents that people bring in the service of helping themselves and others.

Major Concepts

Attending to a group as a system
Education
Focused listening
Informed action
Knowledge as power
Shared leadership
Shared responsibility
Taking a back seat
Talking in the idiom of the other (Middleman & Wood 1990b)

Skills

Become informed
Apply new knowledge
Tune in
Educate the group
Maintain dual focus
Sit on your mouth (Roman 2002)

SKILL (WORKER ROLE): BECOME INFORMED

Elaboration: By *become informed* we mean gather all types of information that can contribute to your decision making as it regards any and every aspect of a group you are planning or with which you are already working.

Principle: Informed action

Theory: Knowledge offers the power to be effective.

Essay: To become informed in work with groups is essential, because you

---

SKILL IN ACTION

Scenario 1. *Thank you for taking the time to talk with me. I understand that you formed and worked with some groups here in the past .... I'd love to hear about them. Can you tell me about them and how they went from your perspective?*

Scenario 2. *I think I just heard Len say that it's really rough going at home, and I saw Andrew and Jon both nod in agreement. Can we hear more about that?*

---

need to establish (while planning) and to keep in mind (during practice) all relevant information related to the group in question. With that in mind, then, to be informed has two components: (1) learning from any number of sources, both internal and external, about your agency's history with groups and its current attitude toward groups and group work and (2) hearing from the people who you might invite to join a group (planning) or who are members of your group (intervention).

Learning about your agency's relation to groups and group work: Not all organizations feel the same way about groups, so knowing feelings, policies, and experiences is a must! A prison system, for example, will have a vastly different perspective regarding the value or formation of groups than will a community center. Further, it is both important and useful to talk with all kinds of agency stakeholders, such as colleagues, program designers, and administrators, all of whom are in a position to answer your questions about *who has done what with groups for whom and when and why in the past and how do they feel about groups now?* Once you know how your work context feels about groups and group work, you can design and plan a service contextually.

Hearing from potential, prospective, or actual group members: The other part to being informed is to learn about the needs and wants of people you call clients, both in planning a group and in conducting your in-service practice (interventions). In planning, the objective is to find out if they would be interested in joining a group and if so, what kind of group and if not, why not? Some people have had negative experiences, while others love the idea of being in a group. In either case, knowing why will help you to design and plan accordingly. Further, once the group is formed you need to make sure that you stay constantly informed about how members are experiencing membership (for example, what they like and do not like and in either case, why). Only by being informed at every moment in your practice can that practice be relevant, supportive, and in sync with all the needs of your work setting. As the saying goes, *knowledge is power* – in this case, the power to make happen what needs to happen in order for your practice to work.

Asking good (the right) questions toward being informed is both a skill (that can be learned) and an art form (that develops with practice), and however you see it, getting answers to the questions you have, requires some thought. First, you have to identify who or what can provide an answer. For example, while some information might come from talking with people in the agency (both representatives and clients) other kinds of information – such as research on groups that have been tried with your client population (or similar groups) – is likely to come primarily from professional literature, such as journals. What is most important is that you exploit all possible sources of information in planning and working with a group so that your practice is carried out in an informed manner within your context rather than perhaps duplicating previous unsuccessful efforts or beginning a group project only to have it curtailed by those who are more "in the know" than you.

SKILL (WORKER ROLE): APPLY NEW KNOWLEDGE

Elaboration: By *apply new knowledge* we mean use the information you have been given to make decisions.

Principle: Informed action

Theory: New knowledge ensures effective decision making.

Essay: Being fully informed and applying new knowledge as a result separates the professional from the technocrat or Good Samaritan. Professionalism relies on being able to understand why one does any given thing. In the case of group work, being informed leads to the possibility of applying new knowledge as we learn all sorts of things from all sorts of places. Agency representatives share history and attitudes about group work, while potential group members share their feelings and histories related to groups along with their needs, goals, and desires. To apply new knowledge in this case means to take into account the information in thinking through what kinds of groups may or may not be possible – that is, in planning and forming a group. When a group is in session applying new knowledge means to incorporate into our own participation what we have learned (heard or seen) since our last intervention. Listening carefully to others, then, and using what we hear to design what we say next is an application of this skill. In other words, whenever we introduce into our practice a statement or action that is based on something that we did not know a moment earlier – we are using the skill of applying new knowledge.

> **SKILL IN ACTION**
>
> *Mmm, Amy said that this place was a real mess over the weekend; there was a fight, and they were short staffed, so I hear it was pretty scary. It's probably on everyone's mind …. I think we should talk about it in group today … how people felt over the weekend, and how they feel now ….*
>
> *Sounds like there was lots of drama. I bet they'll be hard pressed to focus on anything else, at least to begin with.*
>
> *I'm going to bring it up and see where the group is "at;" we can spend the session on it if that will help or whatever time they might want to process what happened and then move ahead. Up to them.*

Differential Application: Once again, this skill is used so often and in so many contexts that we think its differential applications are worth an extra note. The sidebar offers one small example of applying new knowledge in a particular context. However, this skill is used differentially in all kinds of ways, because practice requires all kinds of decisions ranging from the conceptual/theoretical (what kind of group should we have and why or evaluating how a meeting went) to the temporal (size, timing, location, life after group, etc.). When you consider the information you receive from the agency and potential group members to plan a group that fits well within your work context, you are applying new knowledge. When you point out an opportunity for mutual aid (ways in which members might help one another), you are applying new knowledge (by learning about and suggesting a skill or strength that members might share). Finally, as just noted earlier, when you shape or propose particular interventions in group process (by deciding what you want to say or do based on what you just heard), you are applying new knowledge.

In sum, when you consider all of the information you have received from various quarters to inform all aspects of your practice – from planning a group to shaping your own contributions to group process to thinking about life after group for members as they move on and for you and the agency as you evaluate the experience – you are applying new knowledge.

SKILL (WORKER ROLE): TUNE IN

Elaboration: By tune in we mean lean into each moment, listening with everything you already know.

Principle: Mindfulness

Theory: Tuning in to any given moment helps to ensure insight, understanding, and relevance.

Essay: Tuning in is a worker activity that takes place from the very moment that an idea for a group begins to cogitate to the very last moment of participating with group members (thus, even beyond the group meeting). To tune in means to listen to what is said, seen, or heard in a very focused way whether you are actually sitting in a session or while listening to what staff has to say about your ideas for a group or whether a member comes to you to talk about the impact of the group after it has ended. It means to listen in a way that is not distracted and that considers all the factors that may impinge on the message being offered, i.e., the white noise that can accompany a message. In short, whenever you listen in a very focused way, with all your senses including that sense we often call "sixth sense," you are in effect tuning in. You are trying to get a clear grasp of the meaning of what is being communicated. Thus, this means paying close attention to all forms of communication, direct and indirect, verbal and nonverbal and even further, includes close attention to the use of metaphors and other types of language that people use to convey their messages (Middleman & Wood 1990a). If this seems very complicated, just think of it as always paying attention in a very focused way and if even remotely unclear, asking for clarification. Then you will always be on the right path for tuning in.

> **SKILL IN ACTION**
>
> **Scenario 1.** *Joan keeps glancing at Bob while she talks about her son ...*
>
> **Scenario 2.** *Henry seems to be sending us a message with a bit of eye rolling ...*
>
> **Scenario 3.** *It sounds that although you see the benefits differently, you all do want to go in this direction ...*
>
> **Scenario 4.** *It sounds like some differences you're expressing are pretty strong ...*
>
> **Scenario 5.** *It seems that there is quite a bit of judging going on ...*
>
> **Scenario 6.** *You don't all look equally happy with this idea ...*
>
> **Scenario 7.** *You must have some feelings about me, as your new worker ...*

Differential Application: There are several ways of tuning in when listening. For example, when we listen to what is being said in a focused way, we are trying to tune in to what the speaker is trying to convey – not just listening to the surface of the message but also trying to understand if there are underlying messages (latent content, or "reading between the lines"). When we pay attention to non-verbal communication, we are also trying to tune in. For example, noticing and asking about eye rolling or yawning or the fact that a member prefers to sit a little outside the circle or even just keeps on a jacket rather than "settling in" to a session may all be messages that if we pay attention, we can learn something (become informed) and apply it (apply new knowledge) to further the process, individual or group, in a productive way. To consider all relevant factors, such as gender or age or socio-economic status or political ideology or living situation or developmental stage of life, is also an attempt to tune in – that is, to better understand what is being communicated and both the source and impact of the communication.

When we try to anticipate the implications (meaning and impact) of what is being communicated either directly or indirectly and either verbally or non-verbally, we are also trying to tune in. Even further, when we repeat what we think someone just said to be sure that we heard correctly, we are in fact trying to tune in.

Finally, when we use a skill coined by two prominent social work scholars as *talking in the idiom of the other*, we are also trying to tune in (Middleman & Wood 1990a). To *talk in the idiom of the other* has two components. The first component consists of noticing that someone is using a metaphor to communicate something. For example, someone might refer to "never getting to first base." In this case, the metaphor is one of baseball when actually not talking about baseball at all. Or someone might refer to "too many cooks spoiling the broth" when in fact, the person is not at all talking about kitchen etiquette but rather, perhaps, talking about so many people on a team of service or care. Thus, the first component is to notice that someone is using a metaphor to convey something that has nothing to do with the actual content of the metaphor. However, that person is in fact trying to convey something, and so the second component is to either inquire about the metaphor to better understand its application (to become informed) or, if you do understand it, to use the same metaphor to respond (apply new knowledge).

SKILL (WORKER ROLE): EDUCATE THE GROUP

Elaboration: By *educate the group* we mean increase members' knowledge about desirable group norms and values and about their rights, roles, and responsibilities for keeping group process loyal to those norms and values.

Principle: Knowledge as power

Theory: When people know what is expected of them, they can be informed consumers.

Essay: Educating a group takes place throughout the life of the group starting with outreach to potential members, including interviews during which you talk about the group you

---

SKILL IN ACTION

First, let me say that I see you as experts in your own right in this group – in your lives, experiences, and what you need and want from the group.

So as I see it my role is to help you to bring all your knowledge and savvy into the room in a way that's most beneficial to everyone. And I'll do that by being the educator about the "ways and means" of doing that.

My area of expertise here is about ideal group process – keeping good norms and values going at all times.

This may be different from other group experiences you've had …

---

have in mind or inquire about people's needs and talk about how a group might meet those needs, and moves through every stage of group development to the very end (see skill set on group process).For example, you help group members to understand the purpose of the group as its central reference point – the group's North Star, if you will, a point toward which everyone works to reach together or said otherwise, the "why" of the group. You help members to recognize that group direction is not random but rather driven by the relevance and coincidence of their needs, desires, and goals. You also educate them about the values and norms that undergird the kind of group process that is desired in order to help them to share their strengths in helping one another, such as shared leadership, active participation, collective commitment, and open and honest communication.

Educating the group about how to participate in building and shaping group culture is an art form as well as skill, because you educate in a dynamic environment with independent and free-thinking individuals. Thus, your job is twofold: to educate a group about desirable norms and values and to teach group members (explicitly and implicitly) how to keep those norms and values in play at all times. You will know that the group has internalized desirable norms and values when members call one another out if a norm or value is violated – not because the "worker said so" but because the members themselves feel that the "violation" is to the detriment to the group or to one of its members.

In sum, to educate means to carry out a wide array of tasks and interventions throughout the life of a group. At its purest level it is an insistence on the strengths and capacities of group members with the simultaneous willingness of the group worker to cede some authority and control. This stance of reaching for the strengths of group members while refraining from exercising our own ideas all the time (that is, being willing to cede some authority and control) has also been referred to by some in the field as having *faith in the group*. You can only share control over what happens in and to a group if you have faith in the people who are in that group – to begin with, faith that they have strengths and then, faith in their ability and willingness to bring them forth in the service of helping themselves and others in the group.

SKILL (WORKER ROLE): MAINTAIN DUAL FOCUS

Elaboration: By *maintain dual focus* we mean simultaneously pay attention to the group as a system and to each individual group member.

Principle: Attention to the whole

Theory: If you pay attention to the group system as an overall system and to its components as well, you will be attuned to the totality of its function at all times.

Essay: Whenever it might seem that there are two things to which you need to pay attention at the same time, you are in dual-focus mode. Clearly, groups are composed of a number of individuals, just like couples are composed of individuals but are often referred to as "a" or "the" couple or in music, quartets are composed of

---

SKILL IN ACTION

Hey, where are you all? I feel like I'm doing all the work here …. Tom is talking, but the rest of you seem to be zoned out. Here's what I think we need to do. Tom needs to talk to everyone, not just me, and while it may seem strange at first, he needs to move his head around and make eye contact. The rest of us need to ask questions to be sure we really understand what he says and feels.

And as we do that you need to think about your situations and how they are the same or different so we can then compare views. This will bring the whole group into the mix. Okay, let's give it a go. Sorry again for interrupting.

Later: I know you all agreed that a vote would be okay for this decision, but Tom looks quite unhappy …

---

four individuals but referred to as "a" or "the" quartet, both references connoting entities different from/beyond each individual in them. Thus, groups are referred to as "groups," not just "collections of individuals," in order to connote the existence of a system beyond a "bunch" of individuals (Lang 2010) – a system like any other (such as a machine) that has various components.

How the worker belongs to this system is as a catalyst, like the fuel that helps to make an engine run properly. The relationship between individual members and the group as a system is synergistic, with the welfare of each affecting the other. In many machines, if one part malfunctions the entire system breaks down. This is no less true for human systems and in our context, small groups.

The concept of dual focus comes from the world of equestrianism and refers to a rider's need to keep both eyes open to the environment, one eye (hard eye) on the path in front of the horse to watch for immediate obstacles and one eye (soft eye) on the surrounding environs to watch for danger from further afar (Steinberg 2014a). In group work, dual focus is intended to make sure that we keep our eyes on both the group as a system and on the needs of each individual in that system so that we do not care for one at the expense of the other. To elaborate on the sidebar example, here is how it might look in a group to lose dual focus.

- **Losing the individual.** In the sidebar example, while the group as system has agreed to vote and to accept the outcome of that vote, one member appears unhappy. If his feelings are simply ignored, he risks being lost while the group forges ahead on its task without paying attention. This is a moment for some further conversation, one that needs to help the group as a system address the concerns of the individual. If that does not take place, the individual who feels or thinks differently from the others risks feeling invisible and devalued, and the group risks losing that member altogether. Feeling uncared for or misunderstood are common causes of dropping out.

- **Losing the group.** You risk losing the group as a system when you focus on one individual at the expense of the others. This often happens when one person takes the lion's share of speaking, for example, even if in a new group you are happy to have someone – anyone – talk! It is so easy for destructive norms to develop, like a bad habit. However, if one group member has the spotlight without the others being engaged (as in, *Please think about your own situation as you listen and jump in with questions so that we can be helpful*), the group as a group will get lost; it will become a "bunch" of individuals each receiving some kind of help or service from the worker, no longer tied to one another. In fact, experience suggests that most new workers have difficulty with this side of dual focus by doing just that – by engaging in serial interaction with members without bringing the rest of the group into the mix (as in, *Hey, where is everyone anyway?*). The end result is always *casework in a group* (Kurland & Salmon 1992) or the *aggregate therapy of individuals* (Hartford 1971), both of which refer to the fact that interaction is primarily didactic (worker-member-worker) with the group as ghost (silent partner) and thus, no longer reflecting *group* work.

In sum, if you engage at length with one member while others look on and wait their turn, the group system is in danger of being lost as other members become impatient for their "turn" and begin to feel more connected to you and less to one another. At the other extreme, if you simply ignore the feelings or needs of one member, then that person is in danger of being lost as the rest of the members merrily forge ahead. The answer is to engage everyone at all times in all group process (Steinberg 2014a).

SKILL (WORKER ROLE): SIT ON YOUR MOUTH (ROMAN 2002)

Elaboration: By *sit on your mouth* we mean allow a conversation to take place without your input.

Principle: Empowerment

Theory: The less you participate the more others can participate.

Essay: It is often difficult to remain silent when we have ideas, opinions, or suggestions for other people, including people we serve in groups. To sit on your mouth (Roman 2002) does not intend to deny you that opportunity. However, in keeping with the strength-based approach that we espouse, it does intend to allow group members to have center stage in any

---

SKILL IN ACTION

As I think back on the session, I had some pretty solid opinions about the issues and strong reactions to some of the opinions and attitudes in the group …

… but everyone was very engaged, and the talk was animated. No need to interrupt the flow. They expressed how they saw things and why. Of course, I still paid very close attention to the tone of things in case the group needed a little help to keep things cool. But in fact, they did a great job … Good that I sat back!

When we resume next week, I'll have a sense of whether my input would be useful as we move ahead on this. You never know … maybe yes maybe no!

---

helping process no matter the quantity, quality, or potential value of your own ideas. If you, the worker in a clear position of authority, take center stage, then you become the "star" with all other participants as supporting cast. That is not, as we have said repeatedly in this book, group work. It is a way of working with people in groups that keeps the worker as the be-all and end-all of all group process and as such, does not reflect strength-centered practice (Breton 2006; Gumpert & Black 2006; Northen 2006; Northen & Kurland 2001; Steinberg 2014a). The more you talk the less anyone else can talk. Once you (the authority figure in the room) begin talking, what others might have said is often driven underground, especially if those views are even slightly different from yours. The end result of such a scenario is that you are left as the only one talking; the question for practice is then, *Why bother to have a group in the first place?* If the service is just about what you can offer, then you might as well see everyone individually and attend to their respective needs without an audience. However, if you believe that toward the end of a conversation or when everyone else has been heard in full you have ideas that could further advance the work of the moment, then that is a good time to consider offering them to the group with recognition and appreciation for what has already been said and of course, with sensitivity not only to any differences that exist but also sensitivity to how your ideas might be received.

Unit 3:4 Skill Set
Group Process

Overview

The skills in this section, *Attend to Group Process*, all aim to help the worker to conduct practice in a way that introduces participants to, and helps them to sustain, their role as primary movers and shapers of process. Only by sharing authority with you, the worker (which in the context of group process means sharing control over what gets done at each meeting) will group members' strengths truly be identified and harnessed.

Because skills related to group process are inherently about movement, as the term *process* implies, their organization here is worthy of a special note. Please keep in mind as you read this section that the skills described and discussed below could in fact be organized in any number of ways, just as is true of all the behaviors that we identify as skills throughout this book. It may look, therefore, a bit like they are presented sequentially, in step-by-step format; that is, *first you employ this skill, then you employ that skill*. However, please do try to refrain from reading and understanding the application of the skills that we offer here in that way. For example, as you will see when you get to the skill, *evaluation*, that skill is an ongoing activity by both you and the other participants. While we present this skill at the end of this section, it is not an "ending" skill in the category of skills we call *group process*.

In sum, all of the behaviors we offer you in this section are aimed at helping a group to work toward its purpose, however identified. We see these skills as related to initiating, maintaining, and moving group process – whether they entail worker action or actions by other participants, and they can be engaged at any time in the life of a group. We have focused each skill on the context in which it is presented, but you will notice some (inevitable) duplication of action and intent across skills.

Major Concepts

Ambivalence
Agreement
Beginnings
Consensus
Endings
Evaluation
Group development
Group stages

DOI: 10.4324/9781003002789-7

Latent content
Middles
Ownership
Process
Synthesis

Skills

Start the meeting
Secure consensus on work
Confirm consensual agreement
Invite shared ownership
Attend to group stage
Reach for ambivalence
Consider the possibility of latent content
Help the group to problem-solve
Synthesize information received
Evaluate the process

SKILL (GROUP PROCESS): START THE MEETING

Elaboration: By *start the meeting* we mean make a formal delineation between the time the meeting is to begin and the time before it, even if all group members are together beforehand.

Principle: Clarity of action

Theory: The clearer the demarcation of an activity, the easier to separate it from all of the surrounding noise and activity that may (but should not) impinge on it.

SKILL IN ACTION

Good morning. Very glad to see you all here. ... I see you've been chatting already informally, but let's begin our meeting, shall we? ...

Who can recap what we did last week and what we said that we would move to or focus on this week?

Anyone? Everyone?

Essay: It is the worker's job to open each group session formally; this is true even if members have been chatting informally, for example, and even if they have been chatting in a way that speaks to the group's purpose. Just as it is helpful to have a sessional ending when the group reviews and evaluates the work of the day, it is helpful to have a clear start to the work as well. At the very least this allows everyone to begin on a common page, free from assumptions or misconceptions about what is expected. Starting a meeting formally also provides a kind of structure to the process (*We are now beginning the work of this meeting*). In some cases it also helps to keep the content of informal chatter outside the parameters of the meeting (such as gossip, perhaps, often the case with teenagers or people who are in close contact throughout the week). To start the meeting does not imply that the worker "tells" the group what is to be; after a "hello and welcome," starting the meeting might well consist of asking participants what they recall from the previous week, helping to bring their voices into the mix of the day, and helping them to renew their commitment by doing the work of recollection. If no one remembers what happened in the previous meeting, members very likely do not have ownership of the group. In other words, if no one remembers the work of the previous meeting, it likely did not have enough meaning for them to hook into it (i.e., to reflect after the meeting and think about its personal applicability). That is not a good sign, but that said, do be sure to give group members sufficient time to think on it and to come up with a recap; it may take a little time to recall what happened in enough detail to recount it for purposes of beginning this next meeting.

SKILL (GROUP PROCESS): SECURE CONSENSUS ON THE WORK

Elaboration: By *secure consensus on the work* we mean help group members to agree on what to do next (Birnbaum & Cicchetti 2006).

Principle: Explicit and public renewal of commitment

Theory: Collective agreement on what to do next provides direction for group process.

Essay: One very visible way to practice the value of shared group ownership is to reach for consensus about what to do whenever a decision is called for. The context might be as concrete as room temperature or setting up chairs and as complex as changing the entire purpose of a group. These "choice" points are often referred to as "problem solving" in the group work litera-

> **SKILL IN ACTION**
>
> **Scenario 1.** *It's really important that we agree on the agenda so that you always feel this group is for your benefit. If there's a difference of opinion we'll talk it out and find a solution that works for everyone. I don't want to make the decision, and although you could just vote, voting creates winners and losers, and in my experience that's not a good set-up for a small group. Here's why …*
>
> **Scenario 2.** *Last week we agreed to talk at this meeting about the upcoming agency review. As I recall many of you expressed concern about having strangers "lurking about" as you put it, for a week while you come and go.*
> *Is that still our agenda for today either in full or in part?*

ture, and while the issues at hand are not necessarily what we commonly think of as problematic, they do require group decisions. The concept of "problem," then, does not hold a negative connotation; it simply refers to a moment requiring decision. For example, being invited to two holiday dinners at the same time is a problem, but what a lucky "problem" to have!

In democratic societies decisions are often (normally, you might even say) made by a process of voting, and it might seem that voting is also the best or even obvious way to go in any kind of group process. In fact, while voting may be considered one of the fairest ways for collectives of people to make decisions, it comes in a distant second to consensus as a good way for small groups to make decisions, because voting always and inherently creates winners and losers. Therefore, even if all the members of a small group agree to vote on something, some members will come out the "winners," while those whose idea or desire fails will come out the "losers." Much better to do the work of consensus building, a process in and through which every single voice is heard (regarding the whys and wherefores of any possible choice) and in and through which everyone in the group comes to see the value of a particular final choice. In this scenario, everyone has the opportunity to put a case forward, to hear points and counterpoints, and to try to convince co-members of the value of a particular direction.

What is often considered a "downside" to consensus is the fact that it takes time. A vote can take place within a few seconds. Securing consensus, on the other hand, requires time for argument, reflection, and consideration. The "upside" to this process, however, is not just an end result without winners and losers but also that it requires people to think things through together – to articulate, clarify, elaborate, and in many ways communicate so fully that the intent and implications of one's position in the argument are understood. As a side benefit to taking this route for decision making, articulating clearly and fully are excellent life skills that most of us can profit from refining.

Perhaps the most important aspect of this skill, aside from helping people to share their thoughts and feelings in ways that others can understand, is to explain its value at the start of a group in order to prepare members for it. This is especially helpful in a society in which people are very used to a "let's vote and move on" approach to decision making. Once group members understand how consensus achieves both shared ownership of group affairs and a group climate in which no one feels like a loser, they will appreciate the process.

SKILL (GROUP PROCESS): CONFIRM CONSENSUAL AGREEMENT

Elaboration: By *confirm consensual agreement* we mean to make as sure as possible that the consensual decision explicitly agreed to by the group accurately reflects the will of the whole group.

Principle: Protection of people's fundamental right to a voice

Theory: A clear collective commitment offers an accurate starting point for collective action.

Essay: While it is important to explain and help a group to enter into decision making of all kinds with consensus in mind, it is also important to make sure that all voices are, in fact, heard. People are different! Some have no compunction about speaking their minds. Others are shy. Others worry

---

SKILL IN ACTION

Scenario 1. *Okay, so let's take a moment here to make sure that you have said all you want to say about this before we agree finally to go in that direction. Any more thoughts or feelings?*

Scenario 2. *It's important for group good that we get all views out in the open. … Don't feel like you are holding anything up if you speak up. In fact, all thoughts and feelings are helpful by making sure that we cover all bases as we think things through … Much better to hear it all and talk it out now than to have feelings fester as we move along …*

Scenario 3. *We all need to agree on our course of action if what we do is to be meaningful to each of you as members of this group.*

---

about rocking the boat. It is your job to make sure that everyone in the group not only speaks but speaks up; the best way to help to ensure that true voices (what people really think and feel) are heard is to emphasize the value of difference – that it is differences in feelings and viewpoints that really help people to think things through and to make sure that the course of action in any given moment (whether that decision is large or small) fits the bill for everyone.

Can people always agree absolutely about all things at all times? Obviously not! However, there are ways to help accommodate differences so that even if one course of action leaves some group members less than thrilled, asking the group to brainstorm some compromises with which everyone can live, and live without resentment, is a great way to help people to work together and to get their creative juices flowing. For example, one course of action might be undertaken for part of the time with another for another portion of time. Or one course of action might be taken now with another reserved for a later date. Asking group members to come up with acceptable solutions to all of them also highlights your stated desire for them to take responsibility as co-owners of group affairs (see the next skill, *invite shared ownership*) and helps to highlight their strengths as well as they try to figure things out together, each person's idea building on or counterpointing another's.

Differential Application: The skill of confirming consensual agreement is so integral to group process from very beginning to very end that as with some other skills, we think that it merits some special attention here. As noted above, consensus in a group is an important goal for all of its activities that require full participation and full commitment. The very first time you are likely to and should seek consensus is during the beginning-stage activity of *contracting*. A group contract reflects the common understanding among all participants, worker/s and members alike, about the group's purpose (why formed in the first place), about major desirable norms for the group (how it will behave generally with many tweaks and resets to be expected as it moves along), and about its work (what the group will focus on in order to achieve its purpose and within that larger purpose, each member's individual goals).

Another important context for consensus is problem solving, either a group problem (*What should we do now/next?*) or an individual problem (*How can we help Jorge?*). The need for consensus comes into play in this context during the *problem definition* step (Kurland & Salmon 1992; Steinberg 2014a), when the group tries to define a problem that needs attention. It may seem that defining a problem is self-evident; in fact, it is anything but! If you were to ask a handful of people what the problem is regarding climate change, for example, you would get at least that same number of definitions. Furthermore, problems are often defined by a proposed solution! For example, *The problem is that people should be driving electric cars.* Or to come back to the micro level, *The problem is that we need more chairs.* In fact, more chairs is the solution, and in the former scenario driving alternate types of vehicles is also a solution.

Deciphering a problem, therefore, is not simple or straightforward; we often confound the definition with a potential solution or in the case of groups, have difficulty arriving at a single definition on which the group can focus, whether a group-based problem (not enough chairs) or an individual problem (poor social skills). Without accurate definitions, however, there is little hope for solutions that fit the bill; and without consensus on definitions, achieved through explanation and clarification of issues, the ideas that group members bring forth as potential solutions are likely to fly in myriad directions with little focus and thus little helping potential.

SKILL (GROUP PROCESS): INVITE SHARED OWNERSHIP

Elaboration: By *invite shared owner-ship* we mean encourage group members to share the responsibility for what goes on in the group.

Principle: Power in ownership

Theory: Having a stake in something makes one more invested in its success.

Essay: To invite shared ownership in a group accomplishes many social group work goals. First, it reflects your faith in people – that they can (and have a right to) shape their destiny as much as the world and their particular circumstances will permit. Second, it invites the entirety of a person – that is, a *whole* person – into the group, not just the so-called "needy" or "damaged" parts (Breton 2006). Third, it allows

> **SKILL IN ACTION**
>
> *My vision for this group is that we will all share responsibility for what, how, and why we do what we do and ultimately, for this group's success. We all have ideas that can contribute to the work one way or other ...*
>
> *I am not alone in charge here! I bring a certain knowledge and way of thinking from my education and role here, especially about process. But what we actually do and how well you work together will depend mostly on you.*
>
> *You will need to "pull your weight" as co-owners of this group. By that I mean you'll need to share your thoughts and feelings, respond to one another's thoughts and feelings, and bring all the brain power you can muster at any given time to helping us carry out our work.*

you to divest yourself of any notion that you alone are responsible to make or break the success of a group. If others are also responsible for what goes on in the group, then they also share responsibility for success and for failure. This is a huge relief to most new group workers! Fourth, it brings to bear a hefty amount of brain power to any given moment that requires thinking through. It truly reflects in the most positive sense, the *more the merrier* (an oft-cited reason to form a group in the first place) and *strength in numbers* (an important mutual-aid dynamic/see p. 83).

Finally, it helps people (in this case your group members) to confirm their worth in the world, a value that is essential to the good health and welfare of everyone (Breton 2006). There is a theory in sociology called *looking-glass self* (Cooley 1902). Basically, this human-behavior theory says that people end up seeing themselves as others see them (theoretically speaking, we see ourselves as we are reflected in the eyes [eyeglasses/hence looking glass] of others). Thus, inviting group members to share ownership over a group's affairs essentially says to them, *I believe that you can do this, that you should do this, and that you are capable of managing this kind of thing.* As you help group members to in fact do just that, they come to believe it as well, and the synergy of *I can, I should, I will,* and *I can* takes flight, reflecting in a very concrete way the strength-based approach to practice that we are proposing here.

SKILL (GROUP PROCESS): ATTEND TO GROUP STAGE

Elaboration: By *attend to group stage* we mean when thinking about or working with the group, bear in mind its stage of development.

Principle: Respect for evolution

Theory: Recognizing the role and impact of context helps to ensure that everything that takes place respects its context.

Essay: Groups progress from what we generically call "beginnings," pass through what we call "middles," and ultimately find themselves in "endings." Many social group work scholars have delineated specific stages of development (see, for example, Berman-Rossi 1993; Birnbaum & Cicchetti 2006; Garland, Jones & Kolodny 1973; Northern & Kurland

---

SKILL IN ACTION

Scenario 1. *So, this is our second meeting. Let me introduce you to the idea of group development, the framework for how I'm going to think about things here ...*

Scenario 2. *Whoa! Let's stop a bit. It's great to have so many ideas floating! We are clearly moving from "getting to know you" into "middles," which is signaled, you might say, by the feistiness of the talk. That's great; it means you feel easy enough to speak up, even if your view is different. Okay, now deep breath; let's go one by one so we can hear all those ideas ...*

Scenario 3. *We have four meetings left. Let's review what we've done and what we should do with the time left ...*

This has been (a great group), and I will be sad to end!

2001; Papell & Rothman 1980; Schiller 1995, 2007; Berman-Rossi 1993; Steinberg 2014a; Toseland & Rivas 2017; Whittaker 1970). What they all have in common, however, is the recognition that groups have certain characteristics that change over time from the beginning of the first meeting to the end of the last meeting. Here is a glimpse of those characteristics.

- **Beginnings:** At its most basic, when groups are in their beginning stage, members are getting to know one another and the worker (*Who are my co-members, and what will this worker be like?*); spend time trying to figure out how and where they fit into the group (*What is a role for me that feels good and right in this group, and what kind of status will I have?*); and wade through all the initial administrative work (*What is the purpose that we all agree on? How will we behave in this group? How will we interact and contribute? And what will I be able to take from participating?*). Thus, in this stage the members of this "new" group are apt to be on their best behavior.
- **Middles:** As group members come to know one another and decipher how they fit in, they begin to relax, and when that happens "best behavior" also tends to relax. People begin to reveal their true selves – how they really think and feel; and since people are different so too is what they reveal, creating moments of difference that can lead to conflict. The expression of difference does not always lead to what we think of as conflict, but it does always present a fantastic opportunity for people to reflect on their own ways of thinking, being, and doing and to compare and contrast them with those of others, which in turn promotes reflection, rethinking, personal and interpersonal growth, greater insight, and

better understanding. This stage is probably the greatest proportion of a group's lifeline (thus you might think of beginnings and endings each representing (very loosely speaking) about 20% of a group's total lifeline with the balance being spent in middles).

Middles are known to be messy. They are messy because people feel free to talk, to jump in and perhaps interrupt, to get excited or passionate about things, and to dig into new territory both intellectual and emotional. In short, the mess of work replaces politeness (Salmon & Steinberg 2007). In this stage, however, groups are at their most productive, and the mess of it is to be not just tolerated but welcomed and appreciated. You will know that your group is progressing nicely into this stage when people seem more relaxed and ready to jump into the work, offer ideas freely, and take initiative on any number of fronts including what and how to do things.

- **Endings:** Generally speaking, groups eventually come to an end, and a group segues into this stage in approximate tandem with alerts from the worker about the number of sessions left. It is essential that group members be given enough time to navigate this stage; they need opportunities to reminisce, to identify and reflect on what the group has achieved and on what each member has achieved, and generally to evaluate the experience for each person (a process that includes work yet to be done, either in another group or simply in life after group). Endings also encompass the transition from group life to life after group, and it is important to pay attention to what the ending of the group will mean to or imply for each member.

One key to successfully negotiating this stage is to understand that the more meaningful the experience, the more difficult it will be for participants to see the group end, and the more likely they will be to behave in ways that will leave you wondering if the group accomplished anything at all! Just keep that in mind that endings are an emotional time for everyone (most people are not very good at saying goodbye), and make sure to share your own feelings with the group. This is not a time for intellectual analysis. If the group experience was wonderful, sharing feelings is easy. If it was a difficult experience, find something good to say about it, even if you have to reach deep to find something.

SKILL (GROUP PROCESS): REACH FOR AMBIVALENCE

Elaboration: By *reach for ambivalence* we mean invite people to share their mixed feelings.

Principle: Respect for complexity

Theory: Understanding the totality of a picture (situation) enables relevant and significant action.

Essay: To reach for ambivalence is to normalize the complexity of people's feelings around most things in life. People are often anxious about the very same things that excite them. For example, many people have had negative group experiences. While the idea of receiving help or service might be intriguing and even exciting, hope might be mixed with remembrance of past negative experiences. As another example, people may well be of two minds around any number of subjects, so keep in mind that an opinion offered during group process might not contain the entirety of that person's thinking or feeling. To reach for ambivalence, then, means to invite the whole of someone's thoughts or feelings so that every possible angle of any given process of the moment can be given voice, pause for reflection, and ultimately enrich the process. In a nutshell, you might say that if you wish to invite the whole person into your group toward strength-based group process, then you need to know what that "whole" person thinks and feels.

Finally, people's ability to be fully engaged into process is blocked when they are consumed by worries, particularly if those worries remain unexpressed. However, when concerns and fears are aired, they often lose their power. Thus, by discussing ambivalence you also help to diminish people's concerns while increasing their capacity for participation. You create an opportunity to address the content of their anxieties, setting the stage for future process to be both full (all feelings and thoughts welcome) and authentic (what group members really think is acceptable).

SKILL IN ACTION

Scenario 1. *People often have mixed feelings about being in a group. Some have had bad experiences or heard stories from friends or just worry about talking in front of strangers – even if the **idea** of a group seems good. Any of this hit home?*

Scenario 2. *We seem to have identified lots of positives, here. What about other thoughts or feelings? Any worries? Seems to me pretty unlikely that there are just positives and no negatives …?*

Scenario 3. *You've expressed a lot of enthusiasm to opening up the group to a new member, mentioning fresh blood and new thinking … What about the downside of having someone new in an established group? Could there be one?*

SKILL (GROUP PROCESS): CONSIDER THE POSSIBILITY OF LATENT CONTENT

Elaboration: By *consider the possibility of latent content*, we mean listen for undercurrents in all forms of communication, verbal and nonverbal.

Principle: Totality of focus

Theory: Attending to the implicit (indirect) as well as explicit (direct) ensures full attention to what people need.

Essay: As the saying goes, sometimes a cigar is just a cigar. But sometimes a cigar has other meaning to which we refer in human service or counseling work as *latent content*. It is important to not overanalyze every little thing in group process, but it is equally important to keep an ear out, as it were, for communication that arrives between the lines or said otherwise, that is offered as food for thought implicitly rather than explicitly. This is what we mean by latent content. Do not confuse non-verbal communication with latent content, however. Non-verbal communication is actually quite direct, and the messages contained in body language are quite explicit even if they beg a bit of interpretation. Latent content is more subtle; for example, say in the third to last meeting it may not be a coincidence that group members begin to talk about losses and deaths in their families.

Latent content has probably as many definitions as there are individuals trying to understand and address it in their human-service work. What they share in common, however, is that latent content might be said to represent what goes on behind the scenes, to use a theater metaphor, while manifest content (content that is explicit) is what you see on stage. Thus, in the context of group work and group process, you might say that what you hear from members as they work together, hash things out, make decisions, and otherwise engage in all kinds of open process is manifest content – content that is explicit, front and center. In contrast, latent content is what may be being "said," albeit not in words. Perhaps it is expressed through the use of metaphors or themes, or perhaps it is expressed through the use of language that is subtle or nuanced.

The key point is that what you see in group process (what you hear) is not necessarily all there is, which means that you always need be on alert to the possibility that there is "more" to what is going on than meets your eye. This means exercising a very keen ear (often accomplished by trying to tune in [see skill p. 51] to what is being said and seeking clarification the second you are not completely sure about understanding properly) and scanning (see skill p. 11) to make sure that you are in fact catching all there is to catch at any given moment (Brandler & Roman 2015).

That said, if you seek clarification, and the person responding tells you that the cigar is really just a cigar, accept that response. A cigar has the right to be itself, clear and straightforward. To determine on your own that latent content exists when

---

SKILL IN ACTION

Let me think back … Amy described the time her parents forgot to pick her up at camp, Betsy said that she got lost in a mall when she was five, and Carol asked if we had seen the news story about the boy who was placed in nine foster families before the age of five …

I wonder if there may be more here than meets the eye.

You all seem to be recalling stories of loss … I wonder if the group's ending in three weeks is on your minds.

someone insists that what you see is what is meant for you to get is insulting to that person, and it is exasperating to no end to be second-guessed by someone who purports to know you better than you know yourself.

Finally, do not spend so much time analyzing the explicit in order to identify the implicit that you actually miss the point of the manifest content. That is basically a case of tuning out, and while second-guessing oneself can be frustrating, second-guessing others leaves a bad taste in everyone's mouth.

SKILL (GROUP PROCESS): HELP THE GROUP TO PROBLEM-SOLVE

Elaboration: By *help the group to problem-solve*, we mean help group members to make decisions about all the issues – small or large and collective or individual – that confront them.

Principle: Solution-oriented effort

Theory: The more skillful the problem-solving process, the greater the likelihood of positive outcomes.

Essay: Problem solving is something that groups need to do all the time, from the very first moment of their existence to their very end. Problem solving occurs when the group finds itself short one chair; it also occurs when co-members are asked to help address a problem outside of the group. As noted earlier the concept of problem should not be construed as

---

SKILL IN ACTION

Something doesn't feel right ... Some of you are staring down, avoiding eye contact, and not talking much ... Let's be sure about what the problem is ... Let's gather the facts, ask questions, and listen carefully to the person who raised the problem until we think we understand it the same way.

Anyone dealt with a similar situation? Or similar feelings? We want to find common ground here ...

Now that we all "get" the issues, let's look at possible solutions using insight from your own experiences.

Okay, we seem to have an idea; to try out. How to implement it?

As you reflect on this process; what do you each take away?

Okay, let's try it and follow up next week.

---

negative, however. Just think of it as something that requires attention. Thus, problems are simply situations that are open in the sense that they require some kind of action. They come in all shapes, and they come in all sizes.

Problem solving is one of the things that groups do best. No doubt that five "heads" are better than one when it comes to brainstorming possible solutions. The ticket to effective problem solving is to make sure that the issue as articulated in the group is in fact the thing that needs the group's attention – not always an easy task and one that is usually time consuming. If we tackle the issue at face value, we run the risk of defining the real problem incorrectly (Northen & Kurland 2001; Steinberg 2014a; see also Appendix D, *Problem Solving with Mutual Aid in Mind*). Sometimes the way a problem is phrased seems like the problem to address when in fact, it is a symptom of a deeper/different problem that would require a different type of solution. It is always worth the time, therefore, to dig into whatever issue is raised (excluding a missing chair) in order to make sure we get to the root of it (Kurland & Salmon 1993; Salmon & Steinberg 2007). Quickly offered suggestions to solve the problem often result in a "yes, but" response from the person with the problem, and while this may be frustrating to everyone, it is in fact an appropriate response to solutions that are not felt as quite right by the intended recipient. In short, if the actual problem is not accurately defined, then the problem-solvers are working with skewed data that results in misaligned solutions.

Problem solving begins the moment you sense that something is not quite right; something is off in the general everyday flow of things. You may notice a subtle change in the environment or quickly recognize that someone is metaphorically waving a red flag – asking for assistance. *Something doesn't feel right in the group, tonight. I noticed that some of you are staring down, avoiding eye contact, and not talking much.*

For the purposes of explicating this skill set, the problem-solving framework developed by John Dewey (1910), educator and philosopher, is employed below with the addition of a step that brings mutual aid into the picture (Kurland & Salmon 1992) as a way of keeping everyone involved and invested in the process regardless of whose issue the group is addressing.

Step 1: Identify the problem ("something is up"). Worker: *Nobody's talking and lots of you have your arms crossed and coats on. It seems tense in here. Does anyone else notice the tension in the group today?* Marquis: Yes, and I'll say why. It's because Darrel talked about group business to people outside the group and everybody is angry. Worker: *Is that's what's bothering everybody?*

Step 2: Locating and defining the problem. Worker: *Okay. Let's work together to explore the facts. Why do you say that, Marquis?* Marquis: Because Asia told me that Jenny told her that Darrel talked about how we had a big fight in the group. Worker: *Okay, let's talk to each other. Marquis, how about you ask Darrel about this?* Marquis: Right. So, Darrel, did you talk to Jenny about the group? Darrel: No way! I don't talk to anybody about what goes on in this group. That's just wrong. Worker: *But what is the problem here – that we are hearing two sides of a story or that someone may have talked outside the group? Group Members: Both!* Marquis: You know, I know for a fact – and I didn't want to say this before – but I know that Asia likes to cause problems. And she and Jenny are mad at Darrel because he broke up with Asia. (Other group members talk about outside factors and gossip.) Marquis: I think they played me. I'm looking back now and it seems that Asia didn't know details. She just said that she heard we had a fight here. But we didn't have a fight here …. we just disagreed on a few things. (Group members nod) Worker: *Let's assume that Darrel did not say anything, as he has said today. Is there still a problem?*

Step 3: Ask for similar experiences (this step brings mutual aid into the process). Worker: *Okay, so you've identified the problem of outside gossip testing group relationships. Has anyone else dealt with a similar situation?… Or, if not, how about similar feelings to those being shared but from a different experience? We're trying to get to common ground here …*

Step 4: Explore potential solutions. Worker: *Gossip is a topic that's come up a lot in this group? Let's put our heads together and try to figure out some solution to the problem of gossip as it affects this group.* Asia: I think we need to keep an open mind … Don't jump to conclusions. Marquis: Or check in with each other before jumping to the negative. Worker: *So, we're coming up with some solutions here … check first, don't assume, get the facts.* Darrel: Well, we can't control each other, and we definitely can't control the people outside the group. So, we need to communicate with each other.

Step 5: Evaluate potential solutions. *What are your thoughts about the possible solutions we've brought up? How easy or hard will it be to follow through?*

Step 6: Assess implications. Worker: *Okay, we're coming up on the last ten minutes of group. We've been doing some good problem solving today. Does anyone want to recap the solution we're going to test out?* Marquis: Yes, when people talk, we check in with each other, bring it back to the group and be open about it.

Step 7: Test a solution. Worker: *Is everyone willing to test out that new strategy this week if you hear gossip?* Heads nod.

See Appendix D, *Problem Solving with Mutual Aid in Mind*, for an elaboration of this problem-solving model.

SKILL (GROUP PROCESS): SYNTHESIZE INFORMATION RECEIVED

Elaboration: By *synthesize information received* we mean make sense of all information you receive from others.

Principle: Information as power to shape effective effort

Theory: The better, fuller, and clearer the information received the better, clearer, and more secure the direction for "what now."

Essay: The backbone of good synthesis is reflection – reflecting on the

---

SKILL IN ACTION

Okay, so let me see if I can recap … Don suggests that Sara just ignore her boss, right? Jim thinks that Sara should just come right out and say, "Stop it!" Duy thinks that Sara should just quit, and Vanessa and Mercy agree with him. Larry has repeatedly said that Sara should file a lawsuit …

What I'm hearing at the heart of these suggestions is that you are all encouraging Sara to get away from her boss, even if only in her mind. Is that true?

---

meaning and implications of information received. In research this is called qualitative data analysis (Steinberg 2014b). Simply put, as you take in all information available on your subject, you make sense of it, and generically speaking, there are three steps to doing so. First, as you reflect on each bit of information you receive, whether from interviews or reading literature, for example, you consider its effect on your thinking (*How has what I just learned affected my thinking?*). Second, as you reflect on this question you cannot help but compare and contrast what the sources have to say, noting similarities and differences (*Did all the people who responded to me agree on this? Did some disagree? How does the extent of the agreement [or disagreement] affect my thinking now?* or *Does the literature that I have read on this all agree? Are there differences in thinking or in nature or outcome of research? How does it all affect my thinking?*). Finally, as you review those similarities and differences, a story emerges – a general overall perspective on your subject by your sample (i.e., all your sources put together); your self-directed question is then, *What does all this mean in terms of my next action* or *the group's (or group member's) next step? What is the ultimate story that comes out of all this putting together of information?* Once you think you know what that story is, you use words like, "overall," or "primarily," or "in the main" to reflect the predominant sentiment that emanates from the story, always also keeping in mind any differences (Steinberg 2014a and b; Macgowan 2008).

The examples of reflexive process above are based on research; however, the process is exactly the same regardless of context. Whatever the context you synthesize information when you reflect on information received, try to make sense of it, and assign to it some kind of meaning, by which we mean use the whole of it to shape what you do as a next step. In your work with a group this kind of reflection should almost always cause you to share the thinking that comes as a result of it (discretely, obviously, and with sensitivity). In other words, you do not keep your thinking to yourself; you share it so that the whole group can strive to make meaning as well, in this case integrating what you share with what they think (thus, giving them the opportunity to synthesize and integrate information as well). You might also, as another tack, simply echo back to the group what you think you have just heard (information) and work with group members to try to synthesize (make meaning of) the material all together. In other words, you should not reflect then act without regard for the group, such as jump to conclusions. If synthesizing material requires full-group deliberation, then that is the next step after reflecting on what you hear.

In the context of group work, we assume that you started your journey with a premise – a premise that group work has value. As you take in information from many quarters (prospective or potential group members, administration, program directors, and other significant others), the question for reflection might be whether that premise is holding up under scrutiny. For example, is the vision you had for a group the same as it was before you took in all that information, or are your ideas changing as a result of that information? Inevitably, as you gather information a story about needs, purpose, and relevant response (professional action or service) begins to take shape. What you end up with will be the result of your having synthesized everything that was said to you about your idea. Clearly, the more you know about the interplay of all related variables, the better you know the "story" (culture, norms, attitudes, expectations, etc.) in which you are to operate. Then, once you understand that story you are well armed to develop a group service that fits into that story and that is likely, therefore, to meet with approval, support, and success.

Differential Application: Yet again, we encounter a skill that is used so widely that we think it deserves a special note. Synthesizing information is something that we do every single day almost nonstop throughout our day. Without exercising this skill, we would not be able to function! You have probably never thought of this as a professional-practice skill, but when you apply it purposefully, it becomes a skill.

Synthesizing information is neither esoteric nor particularly daunting – although sometimes it is true that making sense of a great deal of information can be challenging. Still, every time we get two opinions on a subject, we try to synthesize them in a way that makes sense to us. How do we feel about each opinion? Do we see validity in both? Whatever the context or issue, responding to the question of where that leaves you is the process of synthesis. Thus, you synthesize (try to make meaning of) information every time you interact with someone or something that provides food for thought. You will use this skill as you plan and try to prepare a group (try to integrate the meaning of all the input you have received for your idea): what potential group members feel, think, and want; how the organizational cast of players with a stake in what you do see you and your role, what they think about your ideas, and how they feel your work will fit with theirs; and finally, all of your feelings about all that. Then, once the group is formed, you will also use this skill every time you listen to and try to help group members make sense of what is being said.

When the group ends, you will use this skill in order to reflect on, review, and make sense of the entire group experience – its formation; goodness of fit with members' needs both to start and as the group evolved; its utility to each individual in the group; the nature and degree of mutual aid that took place; the goodness of fit between the group's purpose and the amount of time allotted to meetings; the degree to which it helped its members to think on and rethink their ways of being, doing, and thinking; and the degree of sustainability – that is, just how well the group seems to have been able to help members carry new skills of being, doing, and thinking into the other life groups to which they belong.

Finally, you will use this skill as you contemplate another group, relying on many sources of information to respond to questions such as, *Should it be similar? If so, why? Should it be at all different? If so, in what way and why so?* You will have, due to synthesizing all of the information that emanates from this group experience (from your evaluation and that of others), a great deal of information in helping you to consider, design, plan, and form your next group – that is, synthesize and to build on what you now know in order to create a successful new venture.

SKILL (GROUP PROCESS): EVALUATE THE PROCESS

Elaboration: By *evaluate the process* we mean help the group establish continuity by inviting a review of process and discussing a direction for the next step.

Principle: Continuity of purpose

Theory: Ongoing evaluation consistently propels the work toward purpose.

Essay: Evaluation of process takes place informally at all moments from the planning stage (what potential members and staff think of your ideas) to beyond the group (what the group achieved or not, why it worked well or did not, and the implications as you see them for each person who participated). At its most basic, evaluation refers to reflecting on the value or implications of any given moment whether behavior, attitude, or feeling. At its most sophisticated evaluation

---

SKILL IN ACTION

Scenario 1. *I have all these views from clients and staff; how does it affect my planning?*

Scenario 2. *Okay, so let's take a look at what you all are saying at this point …*

Scenario 3. *As we begin who can offer a brief recap of last week and what we agreed on for today?*

Scenario 4. *We have 15 minutes left. Let's review what we did and talk about next week …*

Scenario 5. *We've just talked a lot about Sarah's situation. Now let's hear what was most useful to her … and then what each of you takes away from this.*

Scenario 6. *We just tackled a problem that has been bothering most of you. What was helpful about today's process? And was any part of it difficult? If so, how come?*

---

refers to formal methods for helping professionals to understand the value or implications of their work. Sometimes the context is self (*Was I helpful? If so, how, exactly? If not, why not?*). Sometimes the context is other (*Did Maggie meet her goal? If so, what helped her to do that? If not, why not? And if not, now what?*). The central concern is always the same, however: what was/is the impact of your professional interventions? (Birnbaum, Mason, & Cicchetti 2004; Macgowan 2008; Steinberg 2014b)

In today's world evaluation is regarded as a hallmark of professionalism, a process that leads to developing standards of practice and that separates the technician (work by rote) or Good Samaritan (straight from the heart) from the professional, who always seeks greater knowledge toward a better, more advanced and refined ability to do what needs doing (see, e.g., IASWG *Standards of Practice for Social Work with Groups*, https://www.iaswg.org/standards). Somewhere in the middle of the spectrum from very basic to ultra-sophisticated is the context of evaluating group process, and this skill is ongoing throughout a group's life. It can be conducted very formally, as with an experimental research design, or it can be anecdotal, such as open-ended interviews (as in, *So, Group, what does everyone think of what we did today? Let's hear it.*). Both are intended to gather information that will enhance the work either of the moment or going forward. Evaluating group process accomplishes several goals:

1 Evaluating group process helps members to articulate how they feel about its work (of the moment or of the day or so far) assessing for relevance and quality of movement toward the group's purpose and their individual goals.

2 Evaluating group process helps everyone to review what members actually did, how they did it, why they did it that way, and how it went, so to speak.

3 Evaluating group process ties very explicitly and concretely what was done (as in the case of sessional-end evaluation; see Birnbaum, Mason, & Cicchetti 2004) or is being done (in the case of ongoing evaluation) to what came before in (the work of) previous meetings and to what is yet to be tackled, helping to keep all process on track.

4 Evaluating group process helps to identify the ways in which process has or has not been useful, helping to ensure ongoing relevance.

5 Evaluating group process helps members to reflect on and talk about what went on (or is going on), offering an opportunity to brainstorm or to get creative in shaping the future or to innovate new directions for process. While all aspects of evaluation offer opportunities for members to exercise their voices, this aspect offers that most particularly by allowing them to participate actively in shaping group direction.

6 Evaluating group process allows that which has been successful to be highlighted, helping to make it both sustainable and replicable and helping to highlight the mutual aid that has taken place – how much, in what ways, and how it has benefited everyone (or not, as the case may be).

7 Evaluating group process helps the group to make explicit the nature of all of the forward motion as it forges ahead. As the children's game, *Telephone*, so well illustrates, clarity is key to good group communication!

8 Evaluating group process helps each member to understand exactly what is expected in the near future (next meeting) with an eye on the far future (end goal) as well.

9 Evaluating group process, finally and perhaps most importantly (and also probably representing the umbrella under which all of the above values fit) provides the basis for being able to identify and document evidence of a group's success or at the very least, if it was not successful, then a way of documenting the life of the group – its challenges and its outcomes – and to articulate all of that to all interested parties and learn for the next go-around.

In short, evaluating group process offers clarity about where the group is, so to speak, where it has been, and where it is going next and further helps to ensure, maintain, and solidify all process as legitimate vis a vis the group's purpose.

To some extent it can be said that whole-group evaluation (that is, by everyone in the group, not just by the worker) represents informed consent *in vivo* by group members of what is going on in the group, informed consent being a hallmark of strength-centered practice based on the value of self-determination. In fact, there is a form of social research called *participatory action research*, and with some forethought and creative thinking the methods of that form of research could be adapted to or superimposed onto any evaluation of group process (Jacobson & Rugeley 207).

Finally, to assess our work with people is a basic and fundamental mandate of ethical human-service to others – and not just self-assessment but inviting assessment of our work by others, including people we call clients (see, among others, Breton 2006; Brown & Mistry 1994; Gitterman & Shulman 2005; Kurland & Salmon 1993; Macgowan 2008; Magen 2006; Marsiglia 2003;

Middleman 1978; Northen 1998, 2006, Steinberg 2014a; see also IASWG *Standards for Social Work Practice with Groups*, www.iaswg.org/standards and National Association of Social Workers *Code of Ethics*, www.socialworkers.org/About/Ethics/Code-of-Ethics).

Unit 3:5 Skill Set
Mutual Aid

Overview

Mutual aid, a "package" of ways in which people can help one another, is at the heart of strength-based work with groups and therefore, at the heart of this book (Breton 2006; Lietz 2007; Steinberg 2014a). People new to work with groups or people who work with groups but without benefit of education or training do not often know about the beauty of mutual aid and its value to the worker. The beauty of mutual aid is that it identifies ways in which people can help themselves and one another, making the idea of strength-based process a very concrete reality. When you know about the nine dynamics of mutual aid (see below), you understand the ways in which people can work together to achieve their goals, be they large or small.

The value of mutual aid to group work specifically is that it takes the responsibility for group success (usually defined by a group's ability to achieve its purpose or said otherwise, its ability to achieve the reason it meets in the first place) off the shoulders of the worker and distributes that responsibility on to the shoulders of every single participant in the group. *What should we do today?* The worker may initiate that conversation, but group members are responsible in great measure for answering it, as they are for answering the questions, *How are we doing right now? How did we do today?* and *What are we doing tomorrow?*

Not all models of working with groups value the potential of mutual aid, because not all models (like the traditional medical model, for example) are strength based in their perspective regarding what goes on in a group. As noted elsewhere, sometimes organizations place people they call clients into service groups because it makes good c-e-n-t-s rather than professional s-e-n-s-e (See Middleman & Wood 1990a); that is, groups are all about financial efficiency rather than clinical effectiveness. When effectiveness is desired, however, and people are perceived as valuable human-resources, then the worker's role, as noted in the earlier skill category (see worker role, pp. 46–57), is to educate group members about the various ways in which they can help themselves and one another, the upshot being that groups become platforms for mutual aid.

The beauty of mutual aid can be summed up in this way. Mutual aid helps people to not only help themselves and others; it also makes people feel good, a fundamental reason that people choose social service work, for example. Social workers, for instance, become social workers because they want to help people. Why choose a lifetime of helping people? The answer is because to help people makes the person offering the help feel good. Thus, people in groups who are taught (usually by the worker) about the specific ways in which they can be helpful and who take part in

DOI: 10.4324/9781003002789-8

a process where those ways are catalyzed, end up feeling good about being *of value* to others. Synergistically speaking, you might say, then, that feeling valued makes people feel good, which then propels them to try to continue to use whatever skills and talents were identified through the mutual-aid group process to continue on the same track: giving and taking help and as that is taking place, becoming ever more confident in it, competent at it, and happy about it.

The skills in this section all aim to help you, the worker, to understand this very special mindset required for mutual-aid practice and to develop groups into platforms through which people can identify, reach for, and harness each of their particular strengths (skills and talents, including all that is gleaned from life experience) in the service of self-help and help to others.

Major Concepts

Comfort in the company of others
Commonality
Debating differences
Demanding serious attention
Providing support
Problem solving
Self-reference
Self-reflection
Sharing information
Speaking about normally taboo issues
Strength in numbers
Using the group to practice

Skills

Explain mutual aid
Identify group strengths
Harness group strengths
Invite group members to help one another
Evaluate the helping process

Mutual Aid Dynamics: An Overview

Here are the dynamics of mutual aid – nine specific ways that have been identified by social group work scholars and theoreticians (see, e.g., Shulman 2012 and Steinberg 2014a) in which people can help one another, along with a brief proposition about what it means to catalyze each one:

1 **Sharing information.** People help one another by sharing knowledge, ideas, wisdom, experience, feelings, perspectives, and their strengths (skills and talents or ways of being, doing, and thinking that serve them well). To catalyze this way of helping means to ask group members to think about what kinds of information they might hold that if shared, could be helpful to group process.

2 **Debate.** Debating (comparing and contrasting) different ways of being, doing, or thinking can stimulate new ways of looking at old pictures. To catalyze this

way of helping means to ask group members to offer any ideas, viewpoints, or experiences that can help the mix of conversation by offering contrasting food for thought.

3 **Discussing taboo issues.** Permission to raise topics that might be taboo in other groups or social situations often brings great relief and may also result in new helpful ideas. To catalyze this way of helping means to say to a group, *It's okay here to talk about things that may be embarrassing or even feel shameful. This group is for real talk about real concerns that pertain to the purpose of this group. If you need help to do that, I can help you (or we all can).*

4 **All in the same boat.** Being in the company of others who we believe understand us because of shared needs, feelings, experiences, or goals provides help through comfort. Some people worry that common needs will simply sink the boat, but when group process is strength based and not need centered, those strengths are also in the boat and available to lift everyone in that boat. To catalyze this way of helping means to explicitly point out as often as possible what group members have in common – what binds them together in *this* group at *this* time that can help them to advance the group's purpose.

5 **Mutual support.** Mutual support has value in two ways: sympathy and empathy. Sympathy is expressed as understanding because one has "been there" in reality (as in, *I've been in your shoes; I get it.*). Empathy is expressed as having "been there" in spirit, if not in reality (as in, *I've not been in your exact shoes, but I've felt the way I think you feel.*) To catalyze this way of helping means to ask group members to think about their own lives and situations (*self-reflection*) whenever they listen to one another and to refer to their own lives and situations (*self-reference*) whenever they wish to contribute to a helping process – what they did and why it worked well or not so well (Steinberg 2014a).

6 **Mutual demand.** People help one another by demanding that any given moment requiring energy, thought, and focus be taken seriously, a right that belongs to everyone present. To catalyze this way of helping has two parts: (1) model the demand for serious attention to serious things (as in, *Hey, guys, let's refocus!*) and (2) let group members know that they have the same rights and will receive your support to make such demands from one another (as in, *This feels like we're goofing off? Well, then, say something! You all have the right to ask each other to hunker down a bit.*).

7 **Individual problem solving.** To keep mutual aid in play during individual problem solving, the worker asks the members who are listening to engage in self-reflection (*Have I been in such a situation?*) and self-reference (*Let me tell you how I handled it.*) as they try to understand the nature of the problem. These two actions keep mutual aid in play in two ways. First, they keep everyone in the game, not just the so-called presenting person and the worker, because everyone is asked to reflect on their own lives as they listen, creating collective interest and preempting any desire to tune out. Second, they also preempt any temptation to offer advice, an intellectual and non-empathic process that keeps the parties separated on different "moral" grounds (one being the "grand" advisor and the other being the "lowly" recipient). To catalyze this way of helping means to ask group members to be active listeners whenever an individual problem is tackled by thinking about their own lives in order to find either sympathy (same situation) or empathy (same feelings).

8 **Rehearsal.** People help one another as sounding boards for practicing new ways of thinking (a new attitude, for example) or being (a new approach to a relationship, for example), or doing (a new way of carrying out the usual). To catalyze this way of helping means to offer the group opportunities to explore new avenues for addressing concerns, such as role play, for example, or even discussing "what if" scenarios that provide interesting contrast to the usual.

9 **Strength in numbers.** People help one another by lending support, either individual (the group supports a member in taking a particular course of action, such as speaking up to an authority figure) or collective (the group harnesses its collective muscle to take on a piece of social-justice action at any level, such as micro [e.g., organizational], mezzo [e.g., community], or macro [e.g., larger-scale political action]). To catalyze this way of helping means to constantly be on the lookout for ways in which group members can support one another.

The skills in this section, *Catalyze Mutual Aid*, all aim to help a group develop a way of being together that promotes these ways of acting and interacting (see Steinberg 2014a).

SKILL (CATALYZING MUTUAL AID): EXPLAIN MUTUAL AID

Elaboration: By *explain mutual aid* we mean review the dynamics of mutual aid with the group.

Principle: Knowledge as power

Theory: The more people understand what is expected of them, the better they can act accordingly.

Essay: Helping group members to understand the dynamics of mutual aid – that is, the specific and concrete ways in which they might be able to help one another, will go a long way in helping them to understand your expectations. Explaining mutual aid can take many forms, and how you do

> **SKILL IN ACTION**
>
> *I'd like to spend some time talking about the ways in which you can help one another in this group...*
>
> *There is an idea called mutual aid that I think applies here really well. It's sort of a package of ways of helping – nine ways, to be specific, and I'd like to review them with you.*
>
> *While we do that please also think of some examples of how each one might play out here for us in this group. Some might apply more than others, but I bet they will all have a chance in some way or other to be useful here ...*

it exactly will depend on several factors, such as age and cognitive ability of members and purpose of the group. You might wish to type up a brief overview such as the one in this book to share with group members so that they can review and reflect on their own as well as talk about it together. Or you might wish to use language that is very simple and just bring up each dynamic with the group and ask members to think about each one and to offer an example so that they can see the potential of each dynamic "in action" as it relates to them. Whatever way you choose to explain mutual aid, helping group members to understand what you mean by it and how it promotes strength-based process will go a long way in helping them to engage in that process.

In the sidebar the worker uses language appropriate for the group at hand and will allow members to react and respond. In that question-and-answer process it will be noted that some ways of helping may be emphasized in *this* group, while others are de-emphasized or never come into play for any number of reasons. Not everything applies to every group at all times. Most important is to identify the ways in which these people at this time in this group can in fact help one another, and it may well look different in a group of children, for example, than it does in a group of adults.

The term "mutual aid" is often bandied about with assumptions that people understand it in the same way, but that is rarely the case. It is often understood as a "tit for tat" kind of thing: *you help me, I help you.* In fact, as noted in the overall book introduction and also the section introduction, mutual aid is much more subtle than that and is not a quid pro quo interaction. Rather, each person is helped in each interaction, but one person may be helped explicitly while the other is (others are) helped implicitly. The person who receives help leaves the transaction with new ways of looking at old pictures, while the person who did the helping may also leave with new ways of looking at old pictures but even if not, certainly leaves with good feelings and great satisfaction that come with knowing that one has been helpful.

SKILL (CATALYZING MUTUAL AID): IDENTIFY GROUP STRENGTHS

Elaboration: By *identify group strengths* we mean to point out at every opportunity, the ways in which group members are helping one another.

Principle: Informed action

Theory: If you understand the mechanics of what you are doing, you can repeat it.

Essay: Although people are likely to be able to identify those things that they believe they do well, those strengths (skills and talents that are either organic or that have been purposefully nurtured) are not always immediately visible to others. Further, strengths

---

SKILL IN ACTION

When I saw John earlier, he told me about some really good ways of thinking about group project as from past experience.

It would be great if he got the ball rolling on this by sharing his thinking – how he set up the to-do steps and then how they got carried out.

We could then compare and contrast our own needs and figure out our own plan.

John also identified some hassles that he had to overcome along the way ... It would be helpful to hear about those, too.

John, will you get us started?

---

come in a wide variety of shapes and sizes with some more immediately obvious as having potential to help and others, less obvious. For example, the group member who enters the room first and places the chairs in a circle for the meeting is likely to have good organizational or planning skills. The member who always brings a snack in for the meeting is probably very good at (or at least interested in being good at) nurturing. The member who speaks up in meetings is probably admired for being willing to risk exposure of views or opinions or feelings, while the member who is clearly attentive when others speak is probably said to be a good listener. Pointing these out to the group when they happen will help members to be more aware of their own behaviors and how any particular one is helpful to others or in the converse, might be tweaked a bit for improvement. People have other types of strengths too, that are less visible but present and potentially helpful as well. For example, someone with several attempts to stop smoking can be seen (and encouraged) as persistent rather than a failure. Someone who seems to be constantly "knocked about" in life can be seen as someone who keeps getting up and thus, courageous (Steinberg 2014a).

Finally, ways of being, thinking, or doing that might be seen at first glance as negative, like the group member who seems to do all the talking (a "monopolizer") often can be reframed with a bit of thinking. For example, the monopolizer can be seen as someone who is willing to take a risk in sharing feelings or views. That is a positive contribution to group process. True, one would wish everyone to participate, so the question for practice is how to help distribute the process in a way that everyone is in it. In this case, the intervention needs to go something like this, stated to the group while scanning (see skill p. 11): *Hey, where is everyone, anyway? John is doing all the work here!* (followed by the skill, "sitting on your mouth" [see skill p. 57] as people mull over how to jump in).

SKILL (CATALYZING MUTUAL AID): HARNESS GROUP STRENGTHS

Elaboration: By *harness group strengths* we mean ask group members to contribute their skills and talents to the group's work process.

Principle: Strength-centered practice

Theory: Harnessing people's strengths is a way to operationalize the helping process.

Essay: The joy of being helpful is something that brings people to the so-called helping professions. Being helpful makes us feel good about ourselves; we feel like we are making worthwhile contributions to our universe often in small ways and occasionally in a big way. Why, however, one has to ask, should that privilege and honor be given to only helping professionals? Why would the invitation to feel good not be logically extended to everyone?

> ### SKILL IN ACTION
>
> *As we listen to what's going on for Sharon, try to stay in a common feeling state by recalling similar situations or feelings so you can share your own experience and what you did, like if it helped or didn't and why. Hearing what you did or maybe what you wish you had done and why will be very helpful to everyone not only in addressing Sharon's issue but in similar ones in all your lives.*
>
> *For example, seems to me that Bill is never intimidated by authority; that sense could really help here. And Anita has such a warm, easy way with words. Her ideas of how Sharon might speak up in her situation could help. All of you, in fact, will have ideas based on your own strengths and your experiences.*
>
> *Okay, so let's get some more details ...*

In social group work, which is intended to be a helpful, supportive, rewarding, and even joyful experience, helping people to increase their self-esteem is an inherent part of the process (Malekoff, Salmon & Steinberg 2006; Steinberg 2006). One way to do that is to help group members to identify, reach for, and harness (bring forth) whatever they have going for them that can help themselves and others as well – that is, to help them be helpful in a way that feels good. When this happens, the end result is a process that builds confidence, feels creative, offers thanks and praise, and inherently propels renewed optimism for forward motion (strengthened ability to manage life). In practice, then, to harness group members' strengths is to point out at each and every opportunity a particular talent or skill (or savvy) that a member has and that could be used in a helping process. You would not necessarily interrupt a conversation to do that, but when the conversation slows or ends, you would have made mental note of what you heard and point out the ways in which members could help one another.

There are three ways in which you might exercise this skill. One is to simply point out the strengths as they come to the fore through interaction without any particular direction with regard to their use; in this case your aim is to make an explicit point of noting the existence of someone's talent. The second is to point out a group member's strength and direct it to the process of the moment; in this case your aim is to help one member to actually be helpful to another. The third is to bring up a strength that has been noted previously, as the worker does with Anita in the sidebar, and ask that person to keep it in mind as the group engages in a conversation.

In sum, to harness group strengths is to recognize explicitly and bring into play the skills and talents that group members bring with them that could be used to their own benefit and to the benefit of co-members. Note that this skill involves both a thinking piece (listening to what group members have to say or how they behave and making a mental note of what they say or what part of their behavior could help the group) and an action piece (making what you note explicit to the group so that everyone else "sees" it as well and understands its availability for whole-group benefit).

SKILL (CATALYZING MUTUAL AID): INVITE GROUP MEMBERS TO HELP ONE ANOTHER

Elaboration: By *invite group members to help one another*, we mean ask members to listen actively when needs are expressed in case they have ideas about how to be helpful.

Principle: Strength-centered practice

Theory: When people are invited to share their strengths, they take ownership of the process in question.

Essay: As noted in the essay related to the previous skill, to harness strengths means to make a note of all those "being, thinking, and doing" skills and talents that people bring to the group and to make them explicit so that everyone in the group knows about them. This means that the end goal of harnessing group strengths is to have them available for members to

---

SKILL IN ACTION

Scenario 1. *We have this decision to make as a group, and we need to take some time today to think through all the issues, options, and possible outcomes.*

Scenario 2. *So now we've heard Bill talk about the problems he is having with Sue. Having thought about your own situations, let's hear your thoughts. We're not looking at solutions just yet, and no advice, please. What we need at this point is to hear how you all relate to what Bill just shared.*

Scenario 3. *Okay so you've agreed to put together a newsletter about this group and to start that today. Let's build a list of tasks and figure out who's good at what. How can you best share the work to get this done?*

---

use. This brings us to the skill of inviting group members to use those strengths to help both themselves (in meeting their goals) and to help co-members to meet their goals. When group process is such that these skills and talents are clearly the predominant sources of new ideas for being, thinking, or doing, then mutual aid is taking place within the context of strength-centered practice with groups.

What propels this skill is the belief that the "whole" of people should be invited into a group (not just the "needy" parts but also what they have to offer). What results from the skill is a way of interacting in the group that is based on ideas that members offer as new ways of dealing with whatever needs or issues have placed them in this group at this time (Breton 1990 and 2006). Thus, strength-centered practice with groups means to help people to reach for and use (harness) what skills and talents (strengths) they have to help themselves and one another. Group members can be invited to help one another whatever a group's purpose, be it for support or "therapy" or to carry out an administrative task – even to engage in a team sport or put on a play or plan an event, such as an outing.

Finally, it must be said that not only is this a positive, productive, and hopeful way of working with people, it also allows the "work" of helping to be distributed onto the shoulders of all the participants in a group, not just those of the worker. Like anyone, the worker also has strengths that can be harnessed (such as knowing the processes and norms that will best catalyze strength-centered practice), and those strengths can (and should) be shared as the group moves along. The ins and outs of helping in all other ways, however, are shared among all participants so that the worker is never alone in the helping process, removing the burden of being the be-all and end-all of anything.

SKILL (CATALYZING MUTUAL AID): EVALUATE THE HELPING PROCESS

Elaboration: By *evaluate the helping process* we mean invite group members to assess both quantity and quality of help.

Principle: Assessment as baseline for action

Theory: Judgment offers direction.

Essay: What we most want in our practice is to be *relevant*! Sometimes it is called *being on the same page*. We have probably all had the uncomfortable experience of being out of sync with others or with our environment in some way. It is a terrible feeling – like putting enormous effort into a steak dinner only to discover that your guests are vegetarians!

Generally speaking, the primary and most obvious way to assess relevance of service is to find out whether the people being served perceive our service to be in sync with their needs, goals, desires, expectations, values,

> **SKILL IN ACTION**
>
> **Scenario 1.** *As we pause a second I am wondering if how we are talking about Joy's situation is helpful to her. Let's check in to make sure we're on the right track...*
>
> **Scenario 2.** *Okay, so today we talked a lot about ways you can speak up based on how we ended last week ...Was today helpful or not so much?*
>
> **Scenario 3.** *How about sharing your thoughts about what we just did? Any part of it useful? If so, what and how so? Anything not so helpful? If not, what happened?*
>
> **Scenario 4.** *You're probably each going to see our process a little differently. That's fine. What will be very helpful is to get all your points of view.*
>
> **Scenario 5.** *I'd like some feedback on how I got us started today. From your point of view what was most helpful, and what was least helpful?*

etc. In the case of group work, more specifically, this means that you, the worker, ask a group to evaluate its process and progress with questions aimed at finding out if what the group does (process) is helpful and if members perceive that process to be moving the group toward its agreed-upon purpose (progress). Even more specifically, evaluating mutual aid to assess relevance means to find out whether the helping process between among group members is or has been useful.

This means that evaluating mutual aid has two prongs. One prong reaches toward the worker, the overall question being whether the worker is catalyzing (has catalyzed) the kind of inter-member process that has allowed (encouraged and helped) members to help one another. The many sub-questions include whether the worker has consistently reached for and identified group members' strengths, whether the worker has made those strengths and their capacity to help explicit, and whether the worker has encouraged members to actually bring those strengths into the group. Notice in the last sidebar scenario that the request for feedback includes a request for most helpful and least helpful. To ask the question in this way acknowledges that nothing is ever only and always positive and thus, gives permission for criticism. While group members as recipients of your service (in this case, interventions in group process) are generally in the best position to tell you if what you are saying and doing (have said and done) is helpful, it behooves you, the worker, to reflect on this as well. Take the time to think about your own intent (as in, *I wanted to set the stage for the group to help Jane today; did I do that?*), actions (as in, *Did I get out of the way enough for members to actually help her?*), and the outcome of your actions (*What kinds of mutual aid did I see today?*).

The second prong reaches toward group process, the overall question being whether members perceive that what has taken place among them has been helpful. The many sub-questions in this case include exploring the nature of the help (as in, *What kinds of mutual aid have taken place here?*), the ways in which specific members have helped other specific members (as in, *Who helped who in what way and how so?*), and the degree to which that help has been useful not only in the group but in members' ability to participate successfully in other groups to which they belong (e.g., *How has the help you received in/from this group helped you to be a better family member?*). While group members are in the best position to answer these types of questions, the worker, who has witnessed group process, is also in a position to do so but should never be the *only* one to do so. In sum, to ask the members of a group to evaluate quantity and quality of mutual aid means to ask them to join with the worker in judging both the helping process and the worker's actions to catalyze it. Not only does asking group members to evaluate mutual aid express your faith in their ability to rise to that occasion, it confirms your belief in their right to do so as co-owners of the group (Macgowan 2003 and 2008, Steinberg 2014a).

Finally, there is no reason for evaluation to be seen as criticism, even constructive. It is simply a process through which everyone involved gets to have a say in making sure that what happens to them, for them, with them, and even about them remains on target. That is why the more the question of relevance is asked through ongoing evaluation (*Is this moment helpful?*), during process, for example, or at the very least at the end of each meeting, there is much more opportunity to make tiny edits if needed in what the group does next. That way, tweaks can be small, feel non-judgmental (as in, *Oops, we're slipping a little here ...*), and help to keep the group on track by preventing motion into territory that is either tangential to the group's purpose or that moves the group very directly away from its purpose.

Unit 3:6 Skill Set
Conflict

Overview

The possibility of conflict in a group often strikes fear in the heart of even seasoned workers; in fact, the mere *idea* of conflict can strike fear in the uninitiated! Generally, conflict is conjured up as "all hell breaking loose" with people standing up and shouting at one another, perhaps a fist fight, people storming out of the room while others cower in a corner, and in effect, a complete loss of control by the worker. In truth, conflict represents a range of possible actions from politely stated differences of opinion to any version of the above. We propose a completely different way of thinking about conflict, one that welcomes the exploration of its roots and one that approaches it, when it does occur, with some very concrete and specific interventions.

First, the mindset. To begin, we propose that you think of conflict as an expression of difference rather than an unwelcome interruption to be either swept under the proverbial rug (ignored, avoided, delayed) or sledgehammered (shouting over others, trying to prove that someone is wrong or faulty or "bad"). Neither of those work! Ignoring conflict often results in what has been called the "why are you staring at my hamburger syndrome," which refers to a moment in which someone becomes highly annoyed with another for seemingly no reason. In group work you can be almost positive that the "hamburger" represents some kind of unresolved difference – something that someone did or said that is still festering. Rather than clearing the air, sledgehammering thickens it even more by making people feel bad about themselves. When people feel that others see them as "wrong," "faulty," or "bad," there is little chance for maintaining a climate of understanding, insight, and good will for exploring how or why things came to be as they are.

Once you accept conflict as an expression of difference, you will quickly come to see that *precisely* because it does represent difference, it can have some value to a group of people trying to collaborate. Sameness in all aspects of life does not get anyone very far and is not only a completely unrealistic expectation but what we might call "yawn" material, by which we mean that if everyone agreed about everything all the time no new ideas would ever see the light of the day. Even at a dinner table composed of people who all share the same political ideology, for example, it is the nuances of difference that are likely to keep the talk interesting and lively. The same holds true for groups of any kind, including social work groups. In fact, groupthink (when everyone thinks exactly alike) is much more dangerous than difference, because it presents a rigid united front that is almost impossible to break through with an idea that reflects difference, and anyone who tries to do so is likely to be scapegoated and punished.

DOI: 10.4324/9781003002789-9

Thus, we suggest that you reconsider the idea of conflict as an unwelcome or "intrusive" group dynamic and to that end, if you still find yourself fearful, ask yourself the following questions:

1 *In this group, what is the worst that could happen?* Once you have identified that ask yourself the next question.
2 *Is that "worst" that I imagine realistic?* If that worst-case scenario is not realistic, you have won the battle (or at least a good part of it) against your anxiety. If, on the other hand, it is truly realistic ask yourself the next question.
3 *If that did happen, what would I do?* Chances are that with even a minute of thought, you can identify at least one course of action "in case."

Most of the time, in our experience, worst-case scenarios are not realistic but rather the imagination fueling unrealistic fear, usually of losing control. Recall, however, that the entire approach to practice we offer you rests on the expectation and requirement that everyone in a group is responsible for managing group affairs, including the maintenance of good will, respect, and the search for understanding, empathy, and support (Steinberg 2014a). In terms of actual practice, then, recall that you are never ever alone in controlling what happens in and to a group. Control over group process is a shared responsibility of all participants.

One strategy to sustain shared responsibility for control of process during times of difference is to set the stage for it by having said so at the very beginning of the group. For example, you might say:

> *In this group we are bound to have some differences, and when that happens, we will all – every single one of us – be responsible for keeping things respectful. I need each of you to give the group, here and now, that verbal commitment. Let's talk about it, though, before we get to that, because it is essential that everyone understand how important it is that we all share in keeping an eye on things as we move along. Let me begin the conversation by sharing my thoughts about the value of differences so that you can understand where I'm coming from with this expectation, my role in helping things stay respectful when passions rise, and how I will help the group look at its differences in ways that are hopefully helpful …*

The second strategy to help the group to maintain shared responsibility for control of process when differences crop up is to offer gentle reminders about commitment. It can be difficult sometimes for people to hear even (seemingly) minor differences when the nature of that difference feels threatening in some way. One never fully knows how people might be affected by what others consider not very important. Small slights, totally unbeknownst to the one who offered them, have created lifelong enmity. Thus, you will need to offer reminders throughout the process of exploring differences about shared responsibility for and commitment to good will and mutual respect, to open listening, to making clear but softer rather than louder expressions, to honest self-reflection, and to collective attempts at meaning-making (*What does all this difference mean to each of us and to the group as a whole? Can I continue to be a member? Can we continue to work together?*).

Finally, the third strategy is to engage with the skills that we offer you in the following pages: **help the group to expect differences** (so that members will not be shocked, dismayed, or frightened when differences not only crop up but when you say, *Oh, wonderful, we have some grist for our mill; let's look at it!*); **help the group to accept expressions of difference**(*Great, we're getting real now!*); **help the group to see difference as perspective rather than fault or right/wrong**(*Whoops! Let's hold off on accusations and remember that everyone's viewpoint comes from somewhere*); **help the group to talk about differences** (*Whoa! See if you can rephrase that a little more softly so that what you feel can be heard*); and **help the group to make meaning of its differences** (*So now, what do you think this all means for us as a group and for each one of you individually?*).

Major Concepts

Acceptance
Authenticity
Conflict
Difference
Freedom of expression
Group ownership
Insight
Meaning
Perspective
Real talk
Respect
Self determination
Tolerance
Truth as perspective
Understanding
Voice

Skills

Help the group to expect differences
Help the group to accept expressions of difference
Help the group to see difference as perspective
Help the group to talk about differences
Help the group to make meaning of its differences
Address conflict directly

SKILL (ADDRESS CONFLICT): HELP THE GROUP TO EXPECT DIFFERENCES

Elaboration: By *help the group to expect differences*, we mean tell or remind the group that differences are bound to arise when people feel free to be themselves.

Principle: The right to authenticity

Theory: Whenever people are themselves differences are inevitable.

Essay: You know that the group has moved beyond its "beginning" stage when differences crop up. In a new group, people tend to be polite and to agree rather than disagree. Further, in the new group you want to devote more time to finding things for them to agree on than things for them to disagree about. In short, you purposefully seek commonality to solidify their understanding of and commitment to being in this group together with these other people. As the group

> **SKILL IN ACTION**
>
> **Scenario 1.** *I want to bring up the issue of differences. If talk is going to be real, not just superficial or lip service, you're bound to see some things differently. We're new right now and on "best behavior," but with time you're going to get more comfortable to say what you really think. Some of the differences that crop up may be small; some may be large, but no matter, I'll ask that we explore them to see what they mean for the group.*
>
> **Scenario 2.** *Let's halt a bit. Please remember your commitment to mutual respect for the right to speak. It can be hard when we get passionate, but it's so important that what is said gets heard – not so loud as to turn people off and not so soft- like asides or euphemisms – so that what you really mean can't actually be heard. The ticket to working things out here is all of us able to hear all of us ...*

forges ahead, however, and members ease into being themselves because they know one another better, differences will crop up. Some may be around small issues (whether to serve sweet or salty, for instance); some may be around larger issues (how to discipline a child, for example). No matter the kinds of differences that arise, however, it is essential that you anticipate them in any group in which you expect the talk to move beyond polite and superficial.

Because conflict can be the result of passionate differences, it frightens many people – including perhaps the worker. In a preemptory stance, however, it is important that you raise the issue right away in a new group so that members can expect it and not worry unduly about what might happen if they disagree with one another at any given time. It is also important to acknowledge it when the group ventures into territory in which differences seem to be leading to conflict rather than just healthy and happy boisterous debate. By assuring group members that differences are normal in any group and are to be expected and even welcomed as food for thought, you will help the group climate to both become real and stay helpful.

SKILL (ADDRESS CONFLICT): HELP THE GROUP TO ACCEPT EXPRESSIONS OF DIFFERENCE

Elaboration: By *help the group to accept expressions of difference*, we mean ask group members to stay open to one another's viewpoints, attitudes, and feelings.

Principle: Freedom of expression

Theory: Accepting the expression of difference opens the pathway to better understanding.

Essay: As noted throughout this skill set, many people are frightened by the expression of differences in a group, worried that they will lead to some kind of overt fisticuffs. The issue here is that hearing about other ways of thinking, being, or doing can stimulate new ways of living in the world – new and better, more productive or constructive (happier) ways of living and relating. To deny the expression of difference, then, is to deny people opportunities to rethink old ways and to maybe do things better for themselves and for others they care about. The sidebar here offers two types of scenarios in which addressing difference can be helpful. The first one suggests nothing of dramatic importance, but you as worker notice that some differences have been expressed and that exploring them might be useful for the group. Note that the worker in this case assumes that everyone's way of thinking can enrich the group, even if the end result is that no one agrees with it. At the very least it will have offered food for thought. In short, just thinking about (or rethinking) something can be useful! The second scenario offers an intervention when expressions are very heartfelt, perhaps with raised voices, for example, or expressions of frustration. In this case the worker asks everyone to slow down (something that people do not normally do on their own in such instances) and rather than shy away from the bluster, asks everyone to look into each position more fully and more deeply in order to try to understand how such differences could exist in the first place – how people got to be who and how they are. Once we understand how something (someone) came to be, we loathe or fear it less even if we choose to continue to disagree with it.

SKILL IN ACTION

Scenario 1. *This is a good moment to stop and reflect on the fact that we have a couple of different ideas (feelings, approaches) here. That's not a bad thing! It's a good thing - food for thought! Let's hear more about each one and think them through. How might each one advance your own thinking or doing?*

Scenario 2. *Whoa! Wait just a second here! Let's sit back, take a breath, and come at this more slowly. Clearly, we have some dramatic differences. Let's look at them more deeply to try to understand where each way of thinking comes from. And please try to stay open to what each person has to say so that you really hear where that person's coming from.*

SKILL (ADDRESS CONFLICT): HELP THE GROUP TO SEE DIFFERENCE AS PERSPECTIVE

Elaboration: By *help the group to see difference as perspective*, we mean help group members to think about differences not as symbols of right and wrong or fault but as the result of distance between points of view.

Principle: Truth as perspective

Theory: People are the sum of and thus represent their lived experiences.

Essay: It is often the case that when differences arise, people blame one another or consider the other to be at fault or wrong without ever thinking about how that other opinion or feeling state or attitude came to be. Rather, moments of difference are often heated, causing perhaps one person to leave the room abruptly while another shouts an insult and yet another one or two cower in the corner, wishing it would all just go away. None of these actions, however, will ever help people to better understand one another or nurture the possibility of a small but significant change in a view or position that serves its owner poorly. Small-group process, however, under the structured leadership of a worker, can offer people a valuable opportunity to become better listeners, better explainers, and even better people by helping them to learn how people came to be the people they are. Insight and understanding do not necessarily lead to change but usually do lead, at the least, to a more tempered acceptance of "other" (a valuable dynamic in today's multi-cultured world) and in the best-case scenario, to richer relationships.

> **SKILL IN ACTION**
>
> *So, let's look at these different views of the world. Forget about who's right or wrong or who needs to be "corrected." We all have cultures, families, and backgrounds that have led us to where, what, who, and how we are. So, let's try to remember that we don't arrive at who we are in a vacuum.*
>
> *In this case we seem to have quite some distance between the views in this group, so let's try to understand how you came to see things as you do.*
>
> *And please stay away from judgments of right or wrong. Conversion or correction are not the name of the game here. The name of the game is to reach for better understanding, even if it does not lead to agreement.*

Think of it as two people, each on a different side of a river, with a bridge in the middle over the river (of difference). The bridge looks like this:

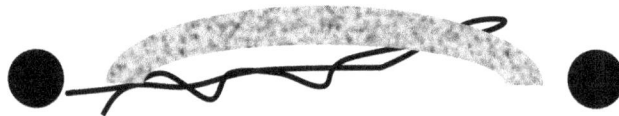

Figure 3.1 Mutual invisibility

As they are, the two people cannot see each other. Your job is to flatten out the bridge to the point at which those two people (in the case of group work, everyone) can see one another's circumstantial, intellectual, emotional, and spiritual territory.

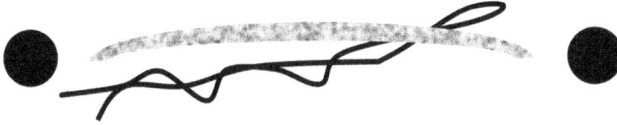

Figure 3.2 Mutual visibility

Once group members can "see" one another, they will be in a better position to reflect on all the ideas, feelings, and attitudes that exist. Your task, then, is to help those ideas, feelings, and attitudes to emerge in a climate of good will, which you will do with the next skill, *help the group to talk about differences.*

SKILL (ADDRESS CONFLICT): HELP THE GROUP TO TALK ABOUT DIFFERENCES

Elaboration: By *help the group to talk about differences*, we mean ask group members to allow one another to express their perspectives.

Principle: Tolerance of different voices

Theory: The expression of difference can lead to better understanding.

Essay: It can be difficult for most people to even listen to someone offer an opinion or take an attitude or "posture" that is vastly different. Even just allowing someone to air something that is considered bad form or taboo (or seemingly mean spirited or prejudiced, for example) sends shivers around. The upshot is that all too often, how people got to think or feel as they do or even just be as they are never gets really understood by others. Rather, people tend to hear one little proposition, often in braggadocio or dogmatic form, and are so turned off that they resist hearing more. The problem with this attitude is that it preempts the opportunity for increased insight and understanding, two things among others that are needed more in the world. In a small group, therefore, in which people have to come together regularly to try for better understanding of any number of things, it is not helpful to simply bury differences or to allow collective fist-banging and hope for the best. All too many groups fall apart precisely because either one or the other happens. Ill will festers, people stop caring about one another, the group becomes haunted by unresolved issues (as in the *Why are you staring at my hamburger?* scenario), and often falls apart completely. Better that a group take the time under the structured guidance of the worker to take a deep breath and allow feelings, attitudes, and opinions to become aired. It is the worker's role to ask group members to constantly ask one another for more information, more clarification, and more explanation about their thoughts until each person can, even if they continue to see things differently, at least understand how each of them came to see things as they do. It is also the worker's responsibility, at least in the beginning, to make sure that everyone both offers and receives input in a respectful manner. Once that norm is set, the worker can ask members to share in that responsibility too as part of its commitment to managing group affairs.

> **SKILL IN ACTION**
>
> *Sometimes it's hard to hear other points of view, especially when they are very different. If we do not listen to one another, however, we'll never understand how someone got to a particular opinion, attitude, or feeling.*
>
> *So at this point, I think what we need to do is move beyond pre-conceived notions and really ask for deep explanations about the "what, why, and how" of each way of seeing things.*
>
> *As we listen to the views expressed, let's ask lots of questions until the speaker feels that we get it. It's not about whether we will ultimately agree or not. It's about the right of everyone to explain how they came to any given mindset, feeling, or attitude.*

SKILL (ADDRESS CONFLICT): HELP THE GROUP
TO MAKE MEANING OF ITS DIFFERENCES

Elaboration: By *help the group to make meaning of its differences*, we mean ask group members to determine the impact of the conversation on themselves, individually, and on the group.

Principle: Group ownership/self determination

Theory: Determining the impact of something provides information to navigate next steps.

Essay: Many people have experienced the end result of conflict as harsh and unforgiving words and behaviors. As noted, differences are what keep a group stimulated and stimulating, but how they are addressed (thought of and talked about) needs to be done in a way that (1) includes everyone in the group (even if the conflict is between only two members) because everyone has a stake in the outcome, (2) maintains a tone of curiosity and respect throughout (rather than derision or dismissal), (3) includes a conversation about how the views or feelings expressed came to be (so that everyone can understand their roots and thus their context), and (4) includes a conversation about the impact of differences on the group. The two central questions for practice here are (1) how does the information shared affect each member, and (2) can the group continue to function as a cohesive group?

In sum, the baseline for practice is that when differences come up, looking at those differences becomes the work of the group at that moment. The expression of difference, even if it leads to a sense of conflict, is not simply an unwelcome interruption into a group's "real" affairs. Looking at the roots of and reason for conflict becomes an important gift that a group can give its members by helping them to learn to ask more fully and think more deeply about people who are very different from them or who live and think in ways that are very different from what they are used to and to do all of that within a context of good will rather than spirit of correction, conversion, or annihilation.

Finally, it is essential that group members hear more, not less, from one another. In direct contrast to the popular "zero tolerance" rule that dominates general western society, the rule of thumb in social group work is "one hundred percent tolerance" – tolerance for people's right to have different feelings and views *even if* the result of conversation is continued full disagreement. Without that tolerance there is absolutely no opportunity for better understanding and insight.

SKILL IN ACTION

So, we've heard these varied and quite different ways of …, and I'm sure you've all had reactions to them. Let's now take some time to think about how they might or might not fit into your own situations.

Maybe we could start with identifying even just one thing you might take from the discussion – maybe a new idea or way of thinking or something you learned.

We can also talk about how something doesn't fit with your situation and why, but let's start with what the conversation might offer. Then we can also talk about the impact of all this on us as a group …

SKILL (ADDRESS CONFLICT): ADDRESS CONFLICT DIRECTLY

Elaboration: By *address conflict directly* we mean help members to confront their differences head on.

Principle: Honest and open communication

Theory: Stunted communication creates fracture.

Essay: Sometimes the expression of differences leads to heat! You probably know what we mean by "heat:" hot heads, hot air, and maybe a hot seat, a scenario in which a group member gets badgered by the rest of the group under the guise of helping that person see the proverbial light. Nothing good can come of any of these dynamics! What a group needs when differences are so passionate as to engender heat is the worker's cool head (so this means that the worker has to see conflict as something useful, not something that should be swept under the rug because it might "disturb the peace").

SKILL IN ACTION

Let's halt a bit. Can someone count to 60?...

Okay, clearly, something is going on, but I'm not really sure what. I have some ideas, but I feel like we're skirting the real issue here.

Let's step back and see if we can identify what is really creating this heat. Lots of back and forth at once going on here, but I'm not sure we are tackling what's really going on.

So, if you all commit to keeping a climate of good will and respect, I know we can figure it out.

Everyone on board, please.

Remember, differences with any real meaning, if swept under the rug, will always (always) return to haunt the group in some way or other, often causing conflict over seemingly minor or trite issues that normally would never cause conflict. Also remember that differences always bring with them some kind or degree of food for thought for everyone present – a chance for viewing, reviewing, and perhaps tweaking their own ways of being, doing, or thinking. Thus, as noted above, what a group needs in times of conflict is communication – open and honest communication, sensitively carried out, and that is where the worker's leadership comes into play. If the group has encountered conflict before, it may well be that members can take on the leadership of addressing it, but to begin with it is the worker's role and responsibility to set the tone, structure, and method for the group to talk things through in a respectful manner and to help group members to make personal and collective meaning of what is heard.

Sometimes, the idea that confronting difference directly can lead to overt conflict makes it frightening to do that initial confronting. One never knows how one's challenge is going to be received. However, since being direct is the only route to the kind of talk through which people can honestly examine the various viewpoints that arise, directness is in fact necessary. This does not mean, obviously, that one has to be either aggressive or adversarial in doing so. As one prominent social work scholar and teacher was often heard to say, being direct – or said otherwise, confronting people's ways of thinking, doing, or being – has the best results when carried out *with an arm around the shoulder*. What this means, in effect, is that one can challenge a way of being or thinking without throwing the baby out with the bathwater, as the saying goes (as in, *I do not care for your thinking because ..., but I do still care about you.*).

It is the worker's role to help group members to do that, perhaps through modeling to begin with but also as the group's primary "educator of norms." As a group matures over time members are likely to get the gist of it and begin to help one another to take up that particular mantle as they address their differences, making it less necessary for you, the worker, to do so.

Endnote

Dear Reader,

We hope you have enjoyed reading this handbook on the skills of social work with groups! Our aim in writing this book was to offer the basics of this social work method to colleagues in the human-service world who currently work with groups, who would like to work with groups, or who are being asked to do so but have not had the luxury of formal training or education in the method.

This method of social work practice that we call social group work is very dear to us. We believe that it embodies the best values of our profession: **Respect for the individual**: the individuality of each member is integral to group work in the ability to harness and lend particular skills and talents that can be useful to others. In fact, real group work places a tremendous value on individuality by seeking and highlighting that which each person can offer others in the way of help. **Self-determination**: as a strength-centered approach to working with people, social group work inherently encourages people to identify and explore possibilities, potential, and consequences rather than impose values and life directions that the practitioner deems appropriate or "correct." **Empowerment**: all actions on the part of the social group worker aim to empower people toward greater ability to manage the vagaries of life from very small "in the moment" challenges to weighty lifetime demands. **Informed consumerism**: by adopting the role of educator, the social group worker devotes all effort to helping people think through and evaluate the consequences of any given way of thinking, being, or doing so that they can be informed consumers. We very much hope that you can see these major professional values reflected throughout the narrative.

Thank you for taking this journey with us. We wish you the absolute best in your professional work. We hope, of course, that your practice will include social work with groups and that the skills and ideas identified in this book will offer you new or perhaps renewed joy in using the social group work method.

Eileen C. Lyons and Dominique Moyse Steinberg

Appendices

Appendix A: On Identifying a Tentative Group Purpose

Max's social work supervisor at a local settlement house has asked him to start a group for children of incarcerated parents. This will be a first-time group for the settlement house and the surrounding community. Max is contemplating the information he has collected from varied sources – practitioners across the country who have formed similar groups, the literature both conceptual and research based, and young people in the program whose parents are actually incarcerated (thus, potential group members).

Max reflects on the youngsters he has already identified as group candidates: seven boys and girls in middle school whose parents are serving prison terms from five years to life. Mulling over a possible group purpose, Max thinks, *This is a sticky wicket. These kids have so many needs!* He considers one possibility: *To help members to adjust to their living situations.* Of the six candidates three live with a grandparent or other relatives, two live with their mothers, and one lives with his father. Several have, in fact, told Max about some of the problems they face in their living situations. For example, Cindy is furious with her grandparents who, she says, treat her like she's the one who committed a crime! Chris says that his mother constantly criticizes him and then says, *You're just like your father. You'll end up in jail, too.* Ishmael lives with his father, who works two jobs, and says that he never gets to talk to his dad because he's missing in action. Ishmael depends on his mother, who is in prison for five years, for normal emotional support during weekly phone calls and occasional trips to the prison upstate. Max remembers how sad he felt when Ishmael said, *When my mother got sentenced, so did I … just no bars.*

So, Max thinks, *the purpose of the group should be to help members to cope with their living situation …. But no, no, that will not work*, Max realizes; *only four members face hardships in this area. That purpose is too narrow.* Then, Max has an epiphany! *What all the kids do need is a caring environment that offers the safety, support, and understanding that a healthy family can provide …. Now there's an idea*, Max thinks. *We'll meet for two hours a week from 5pm to 7pm. We can prepare dinner, then sit down and enjoy the meal together, family-style. We can eat and talk and share what is going on, and they can help one another…Wait … nope! What am I thinking? That is not a group purpose … it's group content …Love the idea of sharing a meal together but that's what we can do, it's not our guiding purpose! Ditto for homework help, playing games, rap sessions – all types of group content– a means to an end – but not the end point. So, let me see, now … the purpose of the group could be to help members to…* Max pauses *… to cope with their lives? No, too general. Plus … coping with life …. Is that the best a group could really do? Couldn't it help to improve and not just "cope?" … Wait! All the kids had mentioned the* *shame they feel about their parents' crimes, the secrets they keep from their friends and teachers.*

Max considers those factors to be central, but there is a broader guiding purpose under which all of that could fit. *These are early adolescents*, Max thinks. *They are struggling to find their identities, clarify values, and fit into social peer groups. As adolescents, they need to separate from families – to develop healthy independence, their own voices. And, they need to be able to make mistakes …*

HAH, Max thinks, *for these kids, mistakes are more than mistakes, they are indictments, because they feel that they've been assigned a kind of "stigma by association" even by their relatives. What a weight*, he thinks. *How about this? The purpose of the group is to help members to find the purpose of their own lives? Oy! Way too grand. One more time. The purpose of the group is to help members to practice feeling free … Too vague, a metaphor. Mmm*, he continues pondering. *Perhaps the purpose of the group could be to help members to feel less alone. Yes*, Max thinks. *Loneliness is a central theme for each of them – alone, burdened, afraid, ashamed. Every moment of their lives is a judgment of them and their situation as children of incarcerated parents. How about this? To feel empowered …. No, that jumps to a solution. How about: To give themselves permission to be who they are. Hmm*, Max thinks, *that may need tweaking, but that could be it.* Under this group purpose (or something very close), every member can find their own voice and sense of agency as they address and solve problems, differentiate themselves from their parents and their parents' choices, and offer compassion for lives that other people's choices dominate. *That's it*, thinks Max. *The purpose of the group could be: To help members give themselves permission to be who they are. This is a great idea to try on for size with these kids*, Max thinks, *but maybe the language should be a little more direct, less conceptual. How about if it was stated like this to the kids: I'm thinking that the purpose of the group would be to help you to be more comfortable and proud of yourself.*

You can see how complicated and somewhat tedious (in the sense of having to think through each idea) it is to move from an original thought about need toward a "final" group purpose! In fact, there is no such thing as simply "coming up" with a group purpose. We often begin by thinking about what people might do together, but what they will do constitutes content (the *what* of a group), not purpose (the *why* of it). It is fine to begin there, of course; anywhere you begin is a good starting point, but the process needs to move to the *why* of bringing people together. Then there is language to consider, feasibility of expectation *vis-à-vis* temporal considerations such as frequency and length of group meetings, and whether achieving the purpose would be acceptable (enough). For example, if a group purpose aims to help member to cope with something, is coping really all you wish them to get from the group? Might the group do better than simply help people to cope? Perhaps to better manage whatever it is, would be more helpful and satisfying. One might be only able to cope in some circumstances, such as those in which any kind of motion or change is not possible; but in most life situations one hopes that one can do better than simply cope. The question for practice is this: Ask yourself for any group purpose statement you come up with, If group members achieve this, will the group actually have achieved what we all hoped it would achieve? And will that be enough? So, for example, if children end up coping better with lousy situations, would that be all right? Probably not so much. That just means learning to live with (accept) the inevitable. Probably the idea of better managing (or even changing) their situations so that things look better (rather than cope with what is) would be more helpful, more uplifting, more rewarding.

In the above scenario, Max arrives at a group purpose that he believes could fit the bill, since all of the children share feelings of shame and stigma from their situations. Now, he will have to try his idea on for size with the candidates to see how they feel about it and take into consideration their input. He may have to tweak the idea altogether, and he may have to change the language such that it reflects their way of thinking and speaking. But at least he has gone through the process that all trained group workers go through in thinking about why would (should) these children get together. So, in the end, here, Max is satisfied enough with his destination and ready to take it to the next step, which is to ask the children for their input – what they think about what he thinks.

Appendix B: On Hidden Agendas

Hidden agendas are the "scourge" of social group work! A hidden agenda refers to the plan that a group worker secretly has in mind for a group (thus, the worker's idea for a group purpose). The key term here is "secretly." The worker has a plan (e.g., for group members to talk about their own childhood in an attempt to get them to reflect on their parenting disciplines), but the members have been told that the purpose of the group is to help them to deal with their children's difficult behaviors.

While this may all look like it does belong in one package, in fact it does not, because the worker's focus will be on encouraging group members to think about and share experiences from their own upbringing, while they will in all likelihood wish to focus on the here and now – on the issues confronting them with their children, on strategies for addressing those issues, and on getting support from the group for the difficulties they face at home.

One can easily imagine a group member, at some point when the group has become comfortable, confronting the worker with an observation something like this: *You keep asking us about how our parents disciplined us, but what we need is ideas for what to do now, with our kids! Why do you keep asking about our past when we need help with the present?!*

This is just one of many examples of a hidden agenda. Why do they exist? Hidden agendas come into play for a variety of reasons. Sometimes the worker, especially a new worker, is afraid to articulate the "real" reason for a group for fear that it will be felt as offensive by potential members. Perhaps it feels impolite or rude to articulate in a direct manner those issues that bring people to service. Or perhaps it feels threatening in some way to identify the issues. Or perhaps the idea of sharing what one knows does not seem that integral to practice.

In truth, people almost always (few exceptions notwithstanding) know very well why they are receiving services, and to hear the worker articulate those reasons out loud, in a posture of sensitivity and care, of course, usually offers a degree of relief (*someone is acknowledging the needs/issues/problems that have brought me to this moment; the talk with this person is straight*). Other times, a hidden agenda crops up because the worker does not either believe in or wish to create a *service-based* relationship with clients (that is, one in which the practitioner's role is to serve the client in a myriad helpful ways). This might be a personal issue (that is, something to do with the worker's own mindset), or it might be somewhat part and parcel of the model of service. Not all models of human-service engage consumers equally; social group work, which is the model we hold dear and that drives this book, aims to engage consumers in all aspects of service to the best of their ability (hence, strength-centered focus and practice); while other models refer to consumers as "patients," intimating a quite unequal relationship between consumer and provider with the provider having the obvious upper hand in all service matters. In those models or practice, the worker takes and retains the role of be-all and end-all of all process, helping and otherwise, with the professional right to judge and make decisions on behalf of the person in need as "patient," who remains in position of recipient of professional expertise. This type of relationship is anathema to social work and in complete contradiction to the field's code of ethics, which requires professionals to work collaboratively *with* people we call clients.

In a nutshell, we say do not create a hidden agenda! Its existence will haunt any group you form and is most certainly in the top few reasons for group failure! Rather, find (practice) ways to articulate sensitively but directly what you see that seems to have brought a person (potential group member) to this moment and how the group you have in mind can help that person.

Here is an example of a hidden agenda in the making but in this case, fortunately derailed by the intern's supervisor.

INTERN: *I've observed tension between Caucasian and African American parents, especially during PTA meetings. In private conversations, African American parents shared their resentment towards the Caucasian parents – especially about their leadership style and vision for the school. My idea is to start a group with the purpose of helping people to build their leadership skills.*

SUPERVISOR: *I'm taking a bit of a leap here, but it sounds like you are hoping that the group will help people of different races to resolve differences.*

INTERN: *Yes, I'm hoping that will come up organically, or I could give it a nudge.*

SUPERVISOR: *Have you thought about directly raising this issue with all involved to understand their viewpoints?*

INTERN: *That might offend people.*

SUPERVISOR: *What you are describing is called a hidden agenda; you have an agenda, but you are hiding it from the people involved. Let's try to deconstruct this a bit …*

Appendix C: On Self-Disclosure

Should I say anything about myself? If so, what should I share? Is it appropriate to share my opinions, experiences, or background if they are similar (or perhaps if they are quite different) from those expressed in the group? How much is all right? How much is too much? Is it even professional to share personal information? What would be acceptable, and what would be "over the line?"

These and many other such questions about self-disclosure crop up all the time among human-service workers, and while there are some guidelines there are really no fast and firm answers. In the following group scenario, the worker shared personal information with members as follows.

PETER: *When I was fired, the bottom fell out from under me. I still haven't found my way back.*

CHUI: *But you were laid off, not really fired.*

PETER: *To my mind it doesn't make a difference. If they wanted me, they would have found a way. I know I'm being hard on myself. One thought cruises through my mind, non-stop: I'm a loser, with a capital L. I can't shake it.*

WORKER: *Can anyone in the group relate to what Peter's saying ... feeling like a loser?*

BERNIE: *Well, that's one hell of a can of worms. We're all here because we all feel like losers.*

AMY: *That's not true! ... Well, maybe.*

The group fell silent.

PETER: *We're the loser club.*

More silence.

WORKER: *(immediately regretting his question about feeling like a loser and feeling a rising sense of panic): Well, you know, I think I may understand something about what Peter's saying ... feeling like a loser when your ego gets kicked around. I was fired once, and yes, for a while, I felt like a loser.*

AMY: *You??*

WORKER: *Yes, me. ... You know, I'm going to push you to help each other and help yourselves to move forward ... past the Capital L.*

SHELLEY: *What happened to you?*

WORKER: *I don't think that sharing all the details of my being fired will be helpful to the group.... but I did want you to know that feeling like a loser after a loss or bad experience isn't a life sentence ... and that I know what it feels like when you don't know or feel that yet.*

PETER: *Well, I guess we've got work to do.*

After the group, the worker wondered, *Did I just jump in and put a bandage on the pain that members were expressing or worse yet, did I show some level of conceit or superiority? Or did my intervention offer a sense of hope that helped the group to move forward?*

Our guideline for making decisions about self-disclosure is actually very simple. It requires you to ask yourself one question. If the answer to that question is such that self-disclosure would enhance (further) your practice goals (the term "your" referring to goals that have been understood and accepted by all involved), then self-disclosure is worth a look. If the answer is such that it would not actually contribute to the help you are trying to offer, then self-disclosure is probably more about meeting your needs than those of your clients (group members). Here is the question to ask yourself: *What purpose would it serve?*

To a great extent, how human-service workers answer these questions will depend on the model of service they follow. Some models of service ask practitioners to refrain from any self-disclosure whatsoever, the rationale being that the service is "all about" the person requiring the service and that sharing personal information of any sort would interrupt (and thus not enhance) the service process. Psychoanalytic models of service would most likely fall into this category of thought. Other models, such as alcohol or drug rehabilitation programs and other programs designed with peer mentoring in mind, encourage self-disclosure, the rationale being that human beings are equal and that engaging in authentic ways as human beings is the most important ingredient. Humanity first, professional service second (or if not second, then highly integrated into a human connection of equality). Services that utilize workers who have experienced the very same issues as the people seeking service often fall into this category, the rationale being that if people seeking service feel understood by someone who has "been there," they are most likely to feel supported enough to do whatever work they need to do.

Social group work, as most (but not all) social work approaches fall somewhere in the middle of these two rather extreme examples. What do you think about the worker's intervention in the above case example, and why?

Appendix D: On Problem Solving with Mutual Aid in Mind
Casework in a Group vs Group Work

As it has been noted in more than one place, problem solving is something that groups do from the moment they meet (*we're short a chair*), and as has also been noted, the concept of "problem" in group work is not a negative one; it simply denotes some kind of issue that needs attention and resolving. That said, groups are also formidable media for the kind of problem solving that is serious – the kind that takes place, for example, when a group member asks co-members to help with some external situation – and this is one of the things that groups do best simply because the proverbial "two brains are better than one" can dominate the process.

What often happens, however, when one group member asks a group for help to address an issue of concern, is what has been coined *casework in a group* (Kurland & Salmon, 1992). What this label refers to is the very kind of problem-solving process that does not – yes does not – rely on group work but takes place in a group anyway. Rather, it is based on a problem-solving interaction between the member requesting help and the practitioner while the other members become onlookers, like a backdrop. Further, it often leads to *serial problem solving*, a process in which members "go" (get the practitioner's attention) one at a time (as in, *Who wants to go next?*).

You can see that casework in a group is not group work, at least not as we understand it, because the group becomes an audience for the worker to practice individual work with one particular group member. You can also see that it does not use the collective skills and talents (strengths) that people bring to a group and might thus be able to contribute toward problem solving, because it is the worker's expertise that takes center stage while others all look on. Finally, you can see why many people who have experienced casework in a group become bored by group membership when it is someone else's turn to "go," often tuning out (daydreaming, napping, etc.) until it is their turn to "go," and even further often having not enough time in that "go" because of course everyone wants a turn!

How to avoid this kind of pitfall? The answer lies in the strength-centered mindset of social group work, which first, expects and even relies on everyone in a group to take an active part in all forms of problem solving and then second, implements that reliance by asking for mutual aid even when the group is focused on one member's issue. Here is how the difference looks in practice, and this difference is what keeps everyone in the group involved at all times, keeps them interested and interesting, and keeps mutual aid in play even when people are looking at one very specific issue for one person.

1 After an agreement to examine an issue brought to the group by a member, the worker makes a brief statement to the effect that everyone is expected to pitch in to the process.

2 The worker then asks members to ask as many questions of that person, as it takes for everyone to be clear about the issue and its extenuating circumstances, including the feelings it engenders. Thus, everyone is closely involved in getting information from that person and further, asking for feelings helps to ensure that members become empathic and stay away from offering intellectual (and usually non-empathic) advice. In fact, advice is a no-no in this process altogether.

3 While this clarification process takes place the worker continuously reminds everyone in the group to think about their own life situations (*self-reflection*, see Steinberg 2014a) as they listen.

4 Once everyone (including the person who brought the issue) believes that enough has been shared to warrant some beginning thoughts on potential solutions (see skill *problem solving*, p. 71), the worker asks group members to share similar situations in their own lives and if none, then to share situations that engendered similar feelings (see *self-reference* in Steinberg 2014a).

The name of the game here is to develop connection and empathy at some level along with ideas for possible resolution, and both successes (what members believe they did well and why) and failures (what they wish they had done better in similar circumstances) are welcome as grist for the problem-solving mill.

As group members share their own experiences, any number of ideas that worked and those that did not work so well come to light, all useful to the person seeking help for thinking about some personal choices and decisions. Further, asking members to jump into the fray with their own experiences and feelings and to stay away from advice maintains equal footing in the group (no one gets a higher status by being the advice-giver) and a climate of empathy all around (everyone's "been there" in some way or other). Finally, that members have the opportunities to reflect on themselves helps them to review their lives (never a wasted effort), makes them feel valued as contributors to the problem-solving process, and maintains a climate of collective interest (for what, after all, is more interesting than oneself).

Problem solving with group work in mind: recognition of group members as potential resources; a reach for, harness of, and active use of all those resources; rewarding for the entire group in so many ways.

References

Berman-Rossi, T. (1993). The tasks and skills of the social worker across stages of group development. *Social Work with Groups*, 16(1–2): 69–81.

Bernstein, S. (1962). Self-determination: King or citizen in the realm of values? *Social Work*, 5(1): 3–8.

——— (1973). Values and group work. In *Further Explorations in Group Work*, S. Bernstein, ed., pp. 145–179. Boston, MA: Milford House.

——— (1993). What happened to self-determination? *Social Work with Groups*, 16(1–2): 3–15.

Birnbaum, M. and Cicchetti, A. (2006). *Working with the Group: Beginning, Middle, and Ending in Each Group Encounter.* Monograph, NY: Wurzweiler School of Social Work/ Yeshiva University.

Birnbaum, M., Mason, S., and Cicchetti, A. (2004). Impact of purposeful sessional endings on both the group and the practitioner. *Social Work with Groups*, 25(4): 3–20.

Brandler, S. and Roman, C. (1995). Uncovering latent content in groups. In *Group Work Practice in a Troubled Society: Problems and Opportunities*, R. Kurland and R. Salmon, eds., pp. 19–31. Binghamton, NY: The Haworth Press.

——— (2015). *Group Work: Skills and Strategies for Effective Interventions* (3rd ed.). New York, NY: Routledge.

Breton, M. (1990). Learning from social group work traditions. *Social Work with Groups*, 13(1): 21–45.

——— (2006). An empowerment perspective. In *Handbook of Social Work with Groups*, D. Garvin, L. Gutierrez, and M. Galinsky, eds., pp. 58–75. NY: Guilford Press.

Brown, A. and Mistry, T. (1994). Group work with mixed membership groups: Issues of race and gender, and social work with groups. In *A Quarter Century of Classics (1978–2004)*, R. Kurland and A. Malekoff, eds., pp. 133–148. Binghamton, NY: The Haworth Press.

Caplan, T. (2005). Active or passive interventions in groups: The group leader's dilemma. *Groupwork*, 15(1): 25–42.

Caplan, T. and Thomas, H. (2003). If this is week three, we must be doing "feelings:" An essay on the importance of client-paced group work. *Social Work with Groups*, 26(3): 5–14.

Cohen, C. and Olshever, A. (2013). IASWG standards for social work practice with groups: Development, application, and evolution. *Social Work with Groups*, 36(2/3): 111–129.

Cooley, C. H. (1902). *Human Nature and the Social Order.* New York, NY: Scribner's.

Coyle, G. (1946). On becoming a professional. In *Toward Professional Standards.* New York, NY: American Association of Group Workers (AAGW now IASWG).

Dewey, J. (1910). *How We Think.* Boston, MA: Heath.

Doel, M. (2004). Difficult behaviour in groups. *Social Work with Groups*, 14(1): 3–22.

Falck, H. S. (1989). The management of membership: Social group work contributions. *Social Work with Groups*, 12(3): 19–33.

———— (1995). Central characteristics of social work with groups – a sociocultural analysis. In *Group Work Practice in a Troubled Society: Problems and Opportunities*, R. Kurland and R. Salmon, eds., pp. 63–72. Binghamton, NY: The Haworth Press.

Galinsky, M. and Schopler, J. H. (1971). The practice of group goal formulation in social work practice. *Social Work Practice*: 24–32.

———— (1972). Warning: Groups may be dangerous. *Social Work*, 22(2): 89–94.

Gambrill, E. (2003). Evidence-based practice: Sea change or the emperor's new clothes? *Journal of Social Work Education*, 39: 3–23.

Garland, J., Jones, H., and Kolodny, R. (1973). A model for stages of development in social work groups. In *Explorations in Group Work*, S. Bernstein, ed., pp. 17–71. Boston, MA: Milford House.

Garvin, C. (1997). *Contemporary Group Work* (3rd ed.). Boston, MA: Allyn & Bacon.

Gitterman, A. and Shulman, L. eds. (2005). *Mutual Aid Groups, Vulnerable and Resilient Populations and the Life Cycle* (2nd ed.). NY: Columbia University Press.

Glassman, U. and Kates, L. (1990). *Group Work: A Humanistic Approach*. Newbury Park, CA: Sage Publications.

Gumpert, J. and Black, P. (2006). Ethical issues in group work: What are they? How are they managed? *Social Work with Groups*, 29(4): 61–74.

Hartford, M. (1971). *Groups in Social Work*. New York, NY: Columbia University Press.

———— (1978). Groups in human services: Some facts and fancies. In *A Quarter Century of Classics (1978–2004)*, R. Kurland and A. Malekoff, eds., pp. 1–8. Binghamton, NY: The Haworth Press.

Henry, S. (1992). *Group Skills in Social Work: A Four Dimensional Approach*. Pacific Grove, CA: Brooks/Cole.

Jacobson, M. and Rugeley, C. (2007). Community-based participatory research: Group work for social justice and community change. *Social Work with Groups*, 30(4): 21–40.

Konopka, G. (1963). *Social Group Work*. Englewood Cliffs, NJ: Prentice-Hall.

———— (1964). Introduction to definition of social group work. In *Working Papers Toward a Frame of Reference for Social Group Work*, M. Hartford, ed., p. 32. New York, NY: National Association of Social Workers.

———— (2008). The significance of social group work based on ethical values. *Social Work with Groups*, 28(3/4): 17–28.

Kropotkin, P. (1908). *Mutual Aid: A Factor of Evolution*. London: William Heineman.

Kurland, R. (2007). Debunking the "Blood Theory" of social work with groups: Group workers *are* made and not born. *Social Work with Groups*, 30(1): 11–24.

Kurland, R. and Salmon, R. (1990). Self-determination: Its use and misuse in group work practice and education. In *Working from Strengths: The Essence of Group Work*, D. Fike and B. Rittner, eds., pp. 105–121. Miami Shores, FL: Center for Group Work Studies.

———— (1992). Group work vs. casework in a group: Principles and implications for teaching and practice. *Social Work with Groups*, 15(4): 3–14.

———— (1993). Not just one of the gang: Group workers and their role as an authority. In *Social Work with Groups: Expanding Horizons*, S. Wenocur, ed., pp. 153–169. Binghamton, NY: The Haworth Press.

Lang, N. (2010). *Group Work Practice to Advance Social Competence: A Specialized Methodology for Social Work*. New York: Columbia University Press.

Lee, J. A. B. (2001). *The Empowerment Approach to Social Work Practice* (2nd ed). New York, NY: Columbia University Press.

Lietz, C. (2007). Strengths-based group practice: Three case studies. *Social Work with Groups*, 30(2): 73–88.

Macgowan, M. (2003). Increasing engagement in groups: A measurement based approach. *Social Work with Groups*, 26(1): 5–28.

———— (2008). *A Guide to Evidence-Based Group Work*. New York, NY: Oxford University Press.

Magen, R. (2006). Measurement issues. In *Handbook of Social Work with Groups*, C. Garvin, L. Gutierrez, and M. Galinsky, eds., pp. 447–460. NY: Guilford Press.

Malekoff, A. (1999). Pink soap and stall doors. *Families in Society*, May/June: 219–220.

Malekoff, A., Salmon, R., and Steinberg, D. M. (2006). *Making Joyful Noise: The Art, Science, and Soul of Group Work*. Binghamton, NY: The Haworth Press.

Marsiglia, F. (2003). Culturally grounded approaches to social justice through social work with groups. In *Social Work with Groups: Social Justice through Personal, Community, and Societal Change*, N. Sullivan, E. S. Mesbur, N. Lang, D. Goodman, and L. Mitchell, eds. pp. 79–90. Binghamton, NY: The Haworth Press.

Middleman, R. (1978). Returning group process to group work. *Social Work with Groups*, 1(1): 15–26.

Middleman, R. and Wood, G. G. (1990a). From social group work to social work with groups. *Social Work with Groups*, 13(3): 3–20.

———— (1990b). *Skills for Direct Practice in Social Work*. NY: Columbia University Press.

Mullender, A. and Ward, D. (1991). Empowerment through social action group work: The "self-directed" approach. *Social Work with Groups*, 14(3/4): 125–139.

Newstetter, W. (1935). What is social group work? In *Proceedings of the National Conference of Social Work*, pp. 291–299.

Northen, H. (1998). Ethical dilemmas in social work with groups. *Social Work with Groups*, 21(1–2): 5–17.

———— (2002). I hate conflict, but …. *Social Work with Groups*, 25(1–2): 39–44.

———— (2006). Ethics and values in group work. In *Handbook of Social Work with Groups*, C. Garvin, L. Gutierrez, and M. Galinsky, eds., pp. 76–90. New York, NY: Guilford Press.

Northen, H. and Kurland, R. (2001). *Social Work with Groups* (3rd ed.). New York, NY: Columbia University Press.

Papell, C. and Rothman, B. (1966). Social group work models: Possession and heritage. *Journal of Education for Social Work*, 2(2): 66–77.

———— (1980). Relating the mainstream model of social work with groups to group psychotherapy and the structured group approach. *Social Work with Groups*, 3(2): 5–23.

Phillips, H. U. (1954). What is group work skill? *The Group*, 16(5): 3–22.

———— (1957). *Essentials of Social Group Work Skill*. New York, NY: Association Press.

Roman, C. (2002). It's not always easy to sit on your mouth. *Social Work with Groups*, 25(1–2): 61–64.

Salmon, R. and Steinberg, D. M. (2007). Staying in the mess: Teaching students and practitioners to work effectively in the swamp of important problems. *Social Work with Groups*, 30(4): 79–94.

Schiller, L. Y. (1995). Stages of development in women's groups: A relational model. In *Group Work Practice in a Troubled Society: Problems and Opportunities*, R. Kurland and R. Salmon, eds., pp. 117–138. Binghamton, NY: The Haworth Press.

———— (2007). Not for women only: Applying the Relational Model of group development with vulnerable populations. *Social Work with Groups*, 30(2): 11–26.

Schopler, J. and Galinsky, M. (1981). When groups go wrong. *Social Work*, 26(5): 424–429.

Schwartz, W. (2005). The group work tradition and social work practice. *Social Work with Groups*, 28(3–4): 69–90.

Schwartz, W. and Berman-Rossi, T. (1990). *The Collected Writings of William Schwartz*. Itasca, IL: Peacock.

Schwartz, W. and Zalba, S. eds. (1971). *The Practice of Group Work*. New York, NY: Columbia University Press.

Shulman, L. (2012). *The Skills of Helping Individuals, Families, Groups, and Communities* (7th ed.). Toronto, CA: Nelson Education.

Steinberg, D. M. (2006). The art, science, heart, and ethics of social group work: Lessons from a great teacher, *Social Work with Groups*, 29(2–3): 33–46.

———— (2014a). *A Mutual-Aid Model for Working with Groups* (3rd ed.). New York, NY: Routledge.

———— (2014b). *The Social Work Student's Research Handbook* (2nd ed.). New York, NY: Routledge

Toseland, R. and Rivas, R. (2017). *An Introduction to Group Work Practice* (8th ed.), London, UK: Pearson.

Trecker, H. B. (1955). *Social Group Work: Principles and Practices*. New York, NY: Whiteside.

Whittaker, J. (1970). Models of group development: Implications for social group work practice. *Social Service Review*, 44(3): 308–322.

Zastrow, C. and Hessenauer, S. (2019). *Social Work with Groups* (10th ed.). Boston, MA: Cengage Learning.

Index

For Product Safety Concerns and Information please contact our EU
representative GPSR@taylorandfrancis.com
Taylor & Francis Verlag GmbH, Kaufingerstraße 24, 80331 München, Germany

www.ingramcontent.com/pod-product-compliance
Lightning Source LLC
Chambersburg PA
CBHW080134270326
41926CB00021B/4481